DATE DUE			

PS-792 FERRETS AND FER RETING,

Title Page:
Although the ferret has a long slender body, it can balance itself
quite easily while sitting up on its haunches.

This book was originally published by David & Charles (Newton
Abbott, London; North Pomfret, VT) under the title *The Ferret
and Ferreting Guide*. © Graham Wellstead 1981.

© 1982 by T.F.H. Publications, Inc. Ltd. for expanded edition. A
considerable amount of new material, including but not limited to
additional photographs, has been added to the original edition.
Copyright is also claimed for this new material.

ISBN 0-87666-938-0

Distributed in the U.S. by T.F.H. Publications, Inc., 211 West Sylvania
Avenue, PO Box 427, Neptune, NJ 07753; in England by T.F.H. (Gt. Britain)
Ltd., 13 Nutley Lane, Reigate, Surrey; in Canada to the pet trade by Rolf C.
Hagen Ltd., 3225 Sartelon Street, Montreal 382, Quebec; in Canada to the
book trade by H & L Pet Supplies, Inc., 27 Kingston Crescent, Kitchener,
Ontario N28 2T6; in Southeast Asia by Y.W. Ong, 9 Lorong 36 Geylang,
Singapore 14; in Australia and the South Pacific by Pet Imports Pty. Ltd.,
P.O. Box 149, Brookvale 2100, N.S.W. Australia; in South Africa by Valid
Agencies, P.O. Box 51901, Randburg 2125 South Africa. Published by T.F.H.
Publications, Inc., Ltd., the British Crown Colony of Hong Kong.

Ferrets and Ferreting

510834

Graham Wellstead

Ferrets belong to the family Mustelidae. They are actually domesticated descendants of the European polecat shown above.

Another member of the Mustelidae family is the stoat (or ermine) at right. Mustelids have the ability to discharge a musk scent from scent glands located near the rectum. This scent is emitted when the animal is frightened or as part of its mating behavior.

Contents

The mink, renowned for its valuable fur, is probably more familiar to most people than its relative the ferret. Unlike ferrets, which are terrestrial, the mink lives both in the water and on the land.

Opposite: Affectionate, playful and curious, ferrets have all the desirable characteristics a pet owner could want. They are small in size, clean, quiet and easy to feed, and they get along well with other pets.

To my wife
PAMELA

Acknowledgments

My grateful thanks go to Michael Clark for permission to reproduce his scraperboard picture of polecats in Brecon Forest and also for his gifts of the polecats themselves. Also to Nick Teall, of the Polecat Distribution Survey, and Brian Martin, Assistant Editor of *Shooting Times* and *Country Magazine,* for permission to use their photographs. Brian's were taken while ferreting with me on a dull February morning when we had more ferrets than rabbits.

Thanks are due too to John Cooper in London and J. T. Lumeij in Holland for their assistance and veterinary advice, and to the many landowners, including Major Shaw of Whitmore Estate, who allow me to practice my art and exercise my various animals and birds.

And particularly thanks to my family: they have put up with the endless chattering of my two-fingered typing as I fought my way through the manuscript.

The white band markings of the badger (above), the ferret (opposite, above) and the wild polecat (opposite, below) are similar. The wild polecat is the animal from which the domesticated ferret was derived.

When tamed, ferrets are highly affectionate creatures who long to be held and loved.

Introduction

This book has been written in the hope that I could pass on some of the practical knowledge and experience I have struggled to extract from the wealth of myth and legend which surrounds the keeping, breeding and working of the domestic ferret. I have striven to break down the barriers of mystery and misinformation in an attempt to show just how easy it really is to keep and work these marvelous animals. The old ferret-keepers were themselves something of a mystery to those outside the circle, and I have lost touch with those who first showed me ferrets when I was a boy. When I later took up ferrets for myself, I discovered an awful truth: the average man knew only the purely basic things. My first ferret was purchased from a man such as this, and my questions about the animal's needs and welfare were met with the comment that there was nothing much to know about ferrets. Having studied animals all my life, I found this unacceptable and set out to learn as much as I could. The going was hard, but I vowed that one day I would become an expert on the subject of ferrets. Since that time ferrets have come right back into popularity, and there are now a great many people seeking good, solid, expert advice.

Now, several years later and after doing research for this book, I am still finding that the more I seek, the more there is to learn. Naturally, I have talked to a great many people, ordinary ferreting men of many years' standing as well as eminent research scientists. However, the greater part of this work is based on my own hard-won first-hand knowledge and experience. I do not claim that my methods of working ferrets are the only correct methods, just that my methods work for me and the others who follow them. Very little information was written down in the past about the keeping and working of ferrets, and almost nothing about their health and welfare was published. Knowledge was passed by word of mouth. Now that chain of knowledge has been broken, so there is a need for the written word to replace it.

CHAPTER ONE The Mysterious Ferret

Of all the animals kept by man, the ferret is certainly one of the least known and the most feared by the general public. In spite of a long history of service to mankind, it is still a much-maligned animal. Over the years I have introduced a great many people to my ferrets, people who have never seen a live ferret before, and almost without exception the first question I am asked is "Do you put them down your trousers?" This strange and meaningless act of bravado, which has tested the nerve of many young men and the patience of many gentle hob (male) ferrets, appears to be the sum total of the average person's knowledge of a very useful and mostly well-behaved animal. In the bad old days (which are not very far away), the ferret was often ill-used and therefore frequently gave as good as it got. It was probably this thoughtless approach to keeping and working ferrets that gave rise to the dubious reputation that still lingers on. Add to this the ferret's snake-like sinuous movement, quick reactions and glittering watchful eyes, and you have the reasons why the animal is close to so many people's subconscious fear-threshold.

The growing body of today's more enlightened ferret-keepers will tell you that if the ferret is treated with the respect and care due to any animal, it will respond by giving many years of friendship and service. The belief that a ferret needs to be savage and half-starved to be of any use when working is, happily, being replaced by the knowledge that a contented ferret will hunt for the sake of it, if not for its owner's benefit. Ferreters do not enjoy pain any more than anyone else, and they can do without having their fingers bitten to the bone by nervous, untrained ferrets.

To me the ferret is a fascinating creature with many points of interest. Its so much more varied uses today than in the past, its growing popularity among new sections of the community and its origins strangely permeated with ill-informed folklore all make it worthy of closer study.

WHAT IS THE FERRET?

Why is the ferret so mysterious? Perhaps because the true origin of the ferret has been in doubt for so many years. Scholars have tried to trace the beginnings of the ferret as a domestic animal, and most have been forced to give up their search for lack of evidence. No one seems to have reached a firm, wholly satisfactory conclusion. Opinions vary, as might be expected, as to what is or was the true ancestor of the ferret and also just when it was first introduced into the British Isles. It had been thought that the ferret was introduced along with the rabbit by the Normans or the Romans. However, recent work suggests that the rabbit was here long before either of these two sets of invaders, and it is reasonable to suppose that the ferret has also been around much longer. Modern thinking is that perhaps the actual animals were already here and that it was the idea of training ferrets which was imported. Ferrets are very popular in southern Europe and North Africa, and, although archaeological evidence is hard to find, it is certain that they have been so for many centuries. In Tunisia ferrets are still kept as pets/pest-controllers and are tethered to a hollowed-out log hung in the rafters or roof space.

As there are no wild ferrets except for feral (escaped) communities, it is fair to assume that the ferret is a domesticated version of one or another of several wild species. But which one? Certainly the ferret is a member of the large and varied family of animals known as the Mustelidae. This family numbers over 60 members in all, of which many are resident in Europe or the United States, including some that are very well-known and widespread as well as others that are rare and endangered. Of the better-known members, the skunks, ermine (stoat), minks, weasels, otters, and badgers are familiar to most people; less known are such creatures as the pine marten and the beech marten. While some of these creatures are perhaps vaguely similar to the ferret, there are others which resemble it much more closely in size and type. It is to these, the Old World polecats, that we should direct our attention.

In Europe there are three distinct species of polecat from which the ferret may have derived: the marbled polecat, *Vormela peregusna*; the steppe polecat, *Mustela eversmanni*; and the European polecat, *Mustela putorius*. We can dismiss the marbled polecat as its gestation period is too long (nine weeks) and its general behavior is quite unlike that of the ferret. In some respects it is closer to the skunk, which is also a member of the Mustelidae, as it is given to throwing its tail forward and standing its ground when attacked, at the same time releasing the contents of its anal scent glands.

The steppe polecat looks a likely ancestor of the ferret, as it is very like a large sandy-colored ferret in its general appearance; however, its lifestyle tends to set it apart. It frequently lives in groups in open country or in semi-desert areas. Its gestation period is slightly shorter than the ferret's, and the young mature much faster—their eyes are open in two weeks and they are weaned in six weeks. Nevertheless, it could still be considered a possibility except for the fact that, as far as is known, steppe polecats have not been interbred with ferrets, and if they were it seems likely that the resultant offspring would be infertile.

We are left then with the European polecat. I cannot see any valid reason to doubt that the ferret is its domesticated descendant. Indeed, I will go further and suggest that the ferret *is* a domesticated version of the wild European polecat. They are so close that colored ferrets (usually known by ferreters as polecats and referred to by me as polecat/ferrets) are often completely indistinguishable from their wild brethren. They interbreed readily, the offspring are all fertile and their chromosome counts are identical. Released from captivity, the ferret (if it survives) quickly reverts and in a generation or two is absorbed into the wild polecat population. There are some small differences in skull measurements when wild and domesticated versions of the animal are compared, but they are so similar that almost all the polecats found wild in Great Britain today are suspect as truly wild stock.

The European polecat, as a wild and free creature in Great Britain, is only found in the more remote parts of western and central Wales. Those that have spread eastward are often considered to be feral ferrets or deliberately introduced, captive-bred wild stock. Those animals found in and around the border counties often seem to have more white on them than specimens from farther west, many having a noticeable throat flash of white hair, which suggests a watering-down of the wild stock owing to polecat/ferret escapees mixing with the lower numbers of truly wild animals. In heavily populated areas very large numbers of ferrets, both white and colored, escape every year. A check with my local police following the escape or unauthorized release and deliberate shooting of one of my own animals revealed that three ferrets are reported *found* every two weeks or—put another way, 78 per year, and that in one suburban town. How many escapees are not found, one wonders? Certainly a great many do not survive for one reason or another.

Pictured here is a "polecat/ferret," or colored ferret. This variety comes in many shades of brown, gray or chestnut.

IDENTIFYING FERRETS—OR POLECATS

A survey into the distribution of the wild polecat in Britain is being conducted by Nick Teall. He is finding the picture extremely blurred and has many years of work ahead of him. The basic difficulty, as you might imagine, is sorting out the truly wild polecats from the feral ferrets. The survey is aided by such things as electron microscopes and is hampered by indiscriminate releases. Nick is always pleased to hear of possible sightings, captures of live animals and bodies of dead ones, no matter how smelly they are provided they are still recognizable. In addition to our mutual interest in the ferret and the polecat, we are keen to hear of any unusual information concerning members of the mustelid group.

We were once galvanized into action when it was reported to us that a man on the east coast had four specimens of the extremely rare—and virtually extinct in the wild—American black-footed ferret. Neither of us had any really detailed information on the animal, but after several telephone calls to experts and a visit to the British Museum (Natural History) we both felt well-enough acquainted with the beast to investigate further. It seems that the American black-footed ferret had last been seen in the wild some ten years before and there is no legal way that four specimens could be owned by a private individual in Great Britain. If the animals really were black-footed ferrets, they would have to be returned to the U.S.A. or there would be an American gunboat steaming up the Medway. With this in mind we shot off to the coast in an attempt to identify not only the animals but also their source.

Our appointment was badly timed in that the wife of the owner was expecting a baby and just before our arrival had started her labor. Although they showed us every kindness, naturally their attention was elsewhere. It was soon obvious that our new friend, a very respectable young man, had no idea of the possible rarity of his charges. As he himself confessed, he had little more than a novice's experience in the world of ferrets. He had, he told us, purchased the animals from the original importer for £20 (about $40) after that man had become bored with them. When we heard this we were almost certain that our journey had been in vain. An inspection confirmed our fears—they were very ordinary polecat/ferrets. The vendor, it seemed, had a silver tongue.

Just in case *you* have to identify the near-fabulous black-foot, let me tell you something about it. It is very much like our ferret in size and build, and its markings are similar to those of the polecat/ferret except that it is rather paler about the body with very dark feet and legs. There is a broad black stripe across the eyes like a bandit's mask, and the black-tipped tail is stoat-like in that it is not colored much above half its length. The ears are larger, rounded but carried higher on the head and face well forward. It is a very attractive creature and one I would much like to include in my own collection should it ever be possible. Its rarity can be attributed to a large extent to the destruction of its natural habitat, the prairie-dog towns of America's mid-west.

Although we had both known in our bones that we were on a wild goose chase, we were just a bit disappointed on our journey home that day. Identification is never easy in any field when your experience is limited, and it can be particularly difficult when it comes to the closely allied members of the ferret and polecat group— some you just have to hold in your hand before you can identify them.

What can often help you to be a little more certain about the identity of the animals, wild or tame, is their general demeanor. As I have already said, ferrets can and do revert to the wild state and seem to achieve the wild animal's awareness in one or two generations, but owners

Many people who see a live ferret for the first time react in fear. Perhaps it's the sharp teeth, the glaring eyes or the quick, sinuous movements that frighten them. But don't judge a book by its cover—ferrets are gentle, docile animals, and a few minutes of observation will dispel all those negative notions.

of captive-bred wild stock agree that it takes rather longer to throw off the mantle of wildness.

The true polecat is in general behavior and attitude a very different animal from the domestic polecat ferret. This is not a comment on its approach to people; the wild polecat can become extremely tame (if that is not too much of a contradiction in terms). My own polecat is so tame that he is generally regarded as a "great kid." I have passed him around a room containing up to 80 people, all total strangers, and he has always been more than happy to accept any fuss going. Indeed, while lecturing to a group of 48 gamekeepers recently, I dropped him on the lap of the nearest man, to be handed around, and, apart from insisting on investigating the poacher's pockets in their jackets, he was no trouble and tamer than many ferrets I have met. The roars of laughter as he shot inside the jacket of each new handler did not bother him in the slightest, any more than the dozens of strange hands which passed him around the room. Yet in spite of this tameness with people, given a situation where he needs to be on his guard he is twice as watchful as any ferret and ten times more agile. He will, given the circumstances, explode into action. One trick which unfailingly terrifies strangers is a daily occurrence. At feeding time he hits the bars of his cage with such force that he seems to be coming straight through—either that or he is going to tear to bits the first hand he reaches. It is all bluster and fun, however, as he will wait for me to take my hand off his food bowl before he eats, making no attempt to bite me or even remove the hand.

The agility of the polecat has to be seen to be appreciated. An artist/naturalist and good friend, Michael Clark, recently lost a newly caught male polecat when it climbed out of a previously "escape-proof" and cleverly designed feeding tube which had foiled the attempts of all his other animals. A ferret does not normally jump up and is very reluctant to jump down from any height over two feet. My polecat and others I know will jump up at least two feet and are always prepared to jump down as much as five feet. I find this remarkable, as my male is a relatively huge animal weighing over four and a half pounds. I do not know of any domestic ferret, large or small, that can compete with that agility or move across the ground at the speed achieved by the wild animal. The first time I used him he went to ground like a rocket. A young ferret used for the first time is usually slow to enter a rabbit hole and will often play around just inside the entrance for a while before either following an adult ferret or plucking up the courage to enter on its own. Not my polecat—he was just in! He killed the first rabbit he met and promptly shot out again to dance about around my feet, full of glee. I thought this was just a case of over-excitement, but he repeats the performance every time. He also seems to take devilish pleasure hunting my dogs, which can be something of a nuisance. Open his traveling box and, if the dogs are in range, he is out after them in a second. At home he ignores them. My long-suffering dogs are, not unnaturally, well-used to ferrets, being virtually brought up with them, and therefore know better than to react to this kind of intimidation. The look on my terrier's face, however, speaks volumes: "Give me a minute or two with 'im, guvnor, and I'll show 'im what 'untin' is all about!" He is not really a lot of use as a working animal but is a pleasure to own and a great character.

THOSE STRANGE "CROSSES"

Occasionally I have come across men who claim to have found the "missing link"—the answer to the ferret's ancestry in the form of "odd" crosses or hybrids which they produce to support their claims. I always try to be polite in these cases as one day they just might be genuine, but I do discount any who claim to have crossed ferrets with cats. More often, the alleged ferret crosses are with other members of the mustelid group, usually the stoat (ermine) or weasel. I have seen one or two ferrets caged with stoats but have yet to see a ferret caged with a weasel. In the case of stoats living with ferrets, the partnership has always seemed uneasy, not to say fragile. Many small (usually sandy-colored) jill (female) ferrets have been handed to me by men who claim that they are stoat/ferret hybrids, but never has there been cause to even half-believe that the animal might really be a hybrid. To me

Ferrets are inquisitive animals, as suggested by this bright-eyed friend who willingly poses for the camera.

and to most of the accepted scientific bodies the cross is most unlikely. We could all be wrong, but none of us will believe in the authenticity of a cross unless we are allowed to examine the hybrid on a scientific basis with all that that involves, including chromosome checks and a possible post-mortem examination of any dead specimen. If this is suggested the claimants tend to back away, muttering darkly about people not believing what they see, and I have yet to be presented with both parents; I am only shown the jill ferret mother. I was once shown an animal which was, it was claimed, a wild weasel: "She's five years old now and has lost most of her color." It was an ordinary sandy jill ferret, and one not even very small; it is hard on such occasions to remain polite. A weasel is a tiny animal that is much smaller than the average ferret and very difficult to keep alive in captivity longer than two years owing to attacks on its brain by parasitic nematodes, as shown by Phil Drabble in his book *Weasel in My Meatsafe*. It is a most unlikely partner for even the smallest ferret. If someone did come up with a genuine stoat or weasel cross, then many of us interested in these animals would be delighted. In all probability, the attempts to produce ferret hybrids and the dubious claims of success are based on the efforts of some ferreters trying to achieve two specific goals; first, to reduce the size of their animals in one generation; and second, to put that little bit of extra zip into them. I will discount the rarity angle, which tends to put the price up when you discuss the possible purchase of one of these so-called hybrids.

For several years now I have had a pipedream of working stoats to rabbits, ferret-style, but I have never been able to obtain any young stoats, in spite of feelers put out among my many keeper friends. Having watched stoats brought up as pets, I suspect that they may not be much use in the field as they are far too quick to control. Released into a closed room, pet stoats will rush around like veritable wall-of-death riders, moving like quick-silver. Domestic ferrets and even my agile polecat appear crippled by comparison. It's a nice little pipedream, though, for one interested in creatures in general and mustelids in particular.

FERRET SIZES

Ferrets vary tremendously in size, and the most highly prized are the small ones. Really tiny ferrets are hard to find; perhaps the people who breed the wee ones are loath to tell and hide them away from prying eyes. I had been brought up to call them whippet ferrets, but a good game-keeper, Frank Goodway, who hails originally from Suf-folk, remembers them being called "snow whites." Frank advertised the fact that he would like to purchase a number of these little ones, but he never got anything resembling the size he was looking for. Small ferrets do have a curiosity value and cost a little less to feed, but I have never worried overmuch about the size of my work-ing jills, provided they can pass through the meshes of a standard purse-net without pulling it down. Over the years I have had one or two whippet ferrets, and indeed I have several now, but even when mated to a tiny hob they tend to produce young which grow to normal size. Although it is possible to breed small ferrets on a regular basis by selection, I have been forced to the conclusion that most have been "fed down" rather than "bred down." Preferring to aim for ferrets of the highest quality in all respects, I have never been tempted to go all-out to pro-duce miniatures.

How do you decide which is a big and which is a small ferret when you have little or no experience? The size varies with the sex to start with, and the average weight must be taken when the animal is reasonably well-fed. A fit (not fat) hob ferret averages around two and a half to three pounds, with the jill averaging one to one and a half pounds. The overall length is something in the order of 20 inches for the male and 12 to 15 inches for the female. Any ferret larger than this can be considered big. The largest ferret I ever heard of weighed six pounds, but he was grossly overweight and could hardly move. The largest I have ever owned weighed over four and a half pounds. He was something like 27 inches long and was all muscle, with no spare weight at all. Far too large to be of much use for either breeding or working, he did have the somewhat unusual advantage of being too big to get over the top of rabbits to kill them, which forced him to drag them out into the open in an attempt to deal with them. This caused him to be regarded as one of the fabled few—a retrieving ferret!

On the other side of the coin, my smallest ferret weighs between six and eight ounces, and she frequently rides her rabbits like the jockey Lester Piggott, very often ending up in the net with them, which can be something of a nuisance. The theory that very small ferrets do not have the strength to kill a rabbit does not hold in practice. They can, of course, get over the top of a rabbit and force it out where a larger animal would fail to move it, but they must be worked for relatively short periods as they tire quickly. In the final analysis I prefer a ferret to be big enough to do the job and work a full day, yet not be so large as to eat me out of house and home or get caught up every time it comes through a net.

COLORS

Not only do ferrets vary in size, but they also vary considerably in color. When referring to a ferret, one usually means the so-called white ferret. It would be more accurate to call it cream, for it is rarely white, more a top-of-the-milk color. In fact, the depth of color varies from almost white to a dark orange-yellow, with all shades in between. Whatever its color, it may be distinguished by its pink eyes, the mark of a true albino. The colored animals (which I refer to as polecat/ferrets to

Ferrets come in a variety of colors, sable (brown) being one of the more common. The sable ferret should not be confused with the American black-footed ferret, a rare and endangered species—although the markings are similar in both animals.

distinguish them from their white brothers and sisters and from the wild variety, the true polecat) come in a great many shades of brown, gray and chestnut. There are two basic color types: normal, which is a dark to blackish brown; and abnormal, a chestnut brown. In both types the body is marked in the same way, with the major color on the extremities. The dark type is dominant, and where a dark parent is used the litter will be of predominantly dark-colored youngsters. They favor their wild ancestors, being black/brown on the feet, legs and tail, with a body color of dark brown guard hairs over a grayish or yellowish undercoat. In some animals the dark guard hair is tipped with silver, giving a gray, badger-like appearance. Very popular now are the red animals known as "sandy" ferrets (or occasionally as polecat crosses), which while not strictly correct is very descriptive. Like the dark form they vary tremendously, going from white with just a hint of color on their feet and tail to a rich auburn. The dark animals are the normal or dominant color type, while the sandy animals are the abnormal or recessive type. If you are going to try and breed for color, you should know that albino mated with albino always produces an all-albino litter; any mating of colored animals to albino produces a mixture of albino and colored youngsters. Sandy animals paired together mostly breed true, with an occasional albino youngster but none of the dark type. The dark animals will produce any combination, but the majority of the offspring are dark.

The recessive "sandy" or "red" polecat does occur naturally in the wild, albeit rarely. I have twice seen skins of the "red polecat ," one a specimen from Tregarron bog— a stronghold of the polecat in Great Britain—and the other from Russia, shown to me in a London furriers. Bearing in mind my earlier comments about the authenticity of any polecat found living wild in Great Britain, one must view the occurrence of red polecats with a certain amount of suspicion. Whatever its background, it is most certainly my favorite; however, my comment about size also holds good for color. Most of us do not care about an animal's color when working—all we ask is that it does its job.

The colored ferret is currently enjoying something of a revival and is very much in vogue, but until quite recently the white ferret was always the first choice of the "old hand." Having originally been produced from the polecat as an albinistic mutation, it became popular because it was so much easier to see while working. If you are really paying attention to what is going on around you it shouldn't matter what color the ferret is. However, wind and rain can completely mask any sound an emerging ferret might make, so if you are working in heavy cover or under laid bracken on a wet and windy day a colored ferret can be difficult to locate. In practice I find the sandy types hardest to follow; one hob I have is almost impossible to spot among dry bracken or leaves—his dark eyes are often the only giveaway. In spite of this disadvantage, the majority of the enquiries I receive for ferrets state a preference for colored animals. It is ironic, though, that every time I find a loose ferret it is colored, almost always a sandy.

HOW FERRETS ARE USED

In the last 40 years or so the ferret has changed from being a pure-and-simple working animal and now takes on other roles. The number of ferrets kept as working animals, although increasing rapidly with the return of the rabbit, runs second to the number kept as laboratory animals. Modern laboratories have found that the ferret is very suitable for many of the drug-screening and drug-production programs which in the past have relied on rats and mice. Ferrets are being used in the screening of new drugs destined to be used during pregnancy, and ferrets were used to produce the vaccine which protects dogs from canine distemper. The drawback with ferrets is that they do not reproduce fast enough. Some research colonies of laboratory ferrets can contain several thousand animals; although sounding vast to the layman, these are small when compared with rat and mouse colonies, even in a small unit. One small colony I know of contained 25,000 rats for use in a single study.

Two other types of ferret-keepers have also emerged: the furbreeder and the pet-owner. Because of the current feeling against the use of real fur as a fashion item, it is unlikely that the ferret will maintain any great value as a fur animal. Mink farms are on the decline for the same reason, but some of those still in existence keep large numbers of ferrets, which they refer to as "fitch," purely for their fur. Nick Teall's father, Dr. John Teall, and I spent a day seeking matched wild skins in the London furriers to make into a fur hat. At one very smart and expensive shop we were shown a magificent fur coat made from fitch. It was incredibly beautiful and incredibly expensive. We were both very impressed and more than pleased that our wives were not with us, for our ferrets might soon have been viewed in a different light.

Ferrets are also becoming increasingly popular as pets. In Canada and the U.S.A. for example, they fetch high prices as exotic pets. In the U.S.A it is almost always against the law to use ferrets as working animals, and therefore those that are kept must live as pets. It is not unusual to hear of them being kept loose in the house together with cats and other animals. One family I know of, living in New York, keeps their much-loved ferrets loose in their apartment; these pampered animals even accompany their owners on vacation to the far west. Almost every week I meet or hear of someone who keeps ferrets as pets in Britain. One large hob ferret lives on a houseboat on the Thames, is given free run of the converted barge and sleeps in a haybag hanging on the end of the boat. The location of his bed changes with the direction of the prevailing wind.

Ferrets make very good pets provided you take sensible and reasonable precautions. *Do not allow young children to handle them without the presence of an adult, and never leave a small child alone with any ferret*, however tame you may think it is! These precautions are no more than any thinking adult would take whenever animals and small children are together.

It is nice to sell ferrets as pets to anyone you think will

No matter how tame your pet ferret may be, never allow anyone (especially young children) to handle it without adult supervision. The ferret has sharp teeth—and a strong grip.

A wild European polecat, *Mustela putorius,* emerging from its burrow.

make a suitable owner, for by doing so you often give people a chance to keep and enjoy the company of an animal which is far more interesting and active than any rabbit or guinea pig. One needs to look for steady, sensible people who do not react to animals in a nervous or neurotic fashion and must make sure that they have the quarters ready and are not impulse-buying. For example, I will not sell to anyone at the summer shows that I attend with my display of ferrets for the Ferret Society. This can upset some of the genuine would-be buyers, but I would rather do that than sell a ferret to the wrong person. I apply the same criteria to the sale of any of my livestock — anyone wishing to buy a ferret, dog or whatever is asked to come to my home or no sale. There are some strange people about with odd ideas about how to care for their animals, whether kept as pets or as workers.

...OR MISUSED

When I look at the advances made in animal husbandry in recent years, I am sometimes lulled into a false sense of security. We have, it seems, come a long way in our treatment of animals. However, the ferret-keepers of medieval times frequently kept their stock in far better conditons than do many of today's enthusiasts. Some ferret-owners would qualify for full-time gainful employment in any torture-chamber worthy of the name — and I could be relied on to give them first-class references. Some of the practices carried out by these types show much more than just an element of misguided ignorance; too often they reveal mindless cruelty. You would imagine that the practice of burning holes in a ferret's lips with a red-hot needle in order to muzzle the ferret by sewing its lips together went out at the turn of the century at the very latest. Not so — I have more than once found loose animals in this condition, and I would dearly like to find the men who did it! Another needless cruelty still perpetrated is the practice of breaking off the carnassial teeth with pliers in an attempt to prevent the ferret from killing rabbits below ground. I can tell you from experience that this does not work. The most troublesome ferret I ever had any dealings with in this respect was a small and very attractive sandy jill who had to be dug out within minutes of entering the burrow. She was a most efficient killer, nailing every rabbit she ever came up to, and she had had all her eye-teeth snapped off short. Obviously she had given trouble before. Her owner passed her on at the end of the season, no doubt to plague some other unsuspecting ferreter—if she lived that long. I had often stressed that she was doomed to an early grave once tooth decay had taken hold unless her broken teeth were pulled by a veterinary surgeon. As usual the reply was that it wasn't worth it for the price of one ferret.

CHAPTER **Confining the**
TWO Brutes—Housing

When housing ferrets, the two watchwords of equal importance are *security* and *space*. Every ferret ever born always wants to be somewhere other than where it is at any given moment, unless it is asleep. Put another way, this means that if it can get out, it will be off. Ferrets are very active animals, and if you want them fit enough to carry out a day's work you must give them quarters in which they can move and take exercise. It is no use having a fortress of a cage which does not allow your ferret to turn round: it will sicken and die at the first opportunity. Nor is it any use having a vast but insecure enclosure, as your pocket-sized Houdini will be out almost before you have turned your back. If you value your animals and also your friendship with your neighbors, you must aim for good-sized quarters which are secure. You like and trust your well-handled, tame and gentle ferret, but you must not expect your neighbors to feel the same way. I live in deepest suburbia, and many of my neighbors believe that I am mad. "There goes that bloke who keeps all those smelly little ferrets and terriers and things," I have heard them say. I sometimes get the feeling that if my stock were to escape I would be driven out of town by a fear-crazed mob, complete with rope and blindfold.

One way to encourage neighbors is to sell or give them a ferret, but that is not always practical. This ploy worked well with my neighbor on one side but not the other. My fellow-ferreter is always prepared to round up any loose ferrets if the need arises. In practice that rarely happens, as any escapees seem to head in the opposite direction, into the garden of a lady who is less than keen on me and who feels even more strongly about my ferrets, in spite of the fact that I have frequently demonstrated just how tame and gentle they really are. Over the years it is almost inevitable that one or two will escape. It is ironic that they should take this direction when it would be easier and much safer to go the other way.

One classic escape was engineered by a large and determined polecat/ferret jill who, just to prove her strength and agility, tore her way out of her cage after discovering a weak spot in the wire. Once she had made a hole big enough to slip through, she dropped four feet to the floor and then climbed out of a window set five feet up in a brick wall. Having overcome what I thought was an impossible barrier and to some extent confounding my theories about the agility of ferrets as opposed to wild polecats, she then burrowed under a close-boarded fence into the ferret-hater's garden. By chance I was home at the time and I knew in my bones what was wrong when I heard the woman shriek my name. This particular jill was normally quite well-behaved, but she had not long ago finished rearing a litter, and this does tend to make a jill super-active and keen to get on with some work. Like all my ferrets she loved a game with the broom I use to sweep out the shed at cleaning time, and it just so happened that my neighbor was sweeping her garden path when my jill made a break for it. Out of the flowerbed she bounced, always ready for a game. Madam, not knowing the animal's intention, promptly struck her with the broom. This was not what the jill had been brought up to expect, and when she was struck a second time she decided to do something about it. Hissing and spitting in full battle order, she drove the terrified woman backward up her garden path and through her French windows. I managed to retrieve the ferret before either party was damaged, but my neighbor was not pleased and it was several weeks before my ferret forgave me.

On another occasion one of my favorite white jills escaped and was found outside the door of the pub just up the road from my home. I had no idea where she had gone until several weeks later when I heard that she had been found and picked up by a young lady who had petted and fussed over her without knowing what kind of animal she was. The girl told me afterward that had she known at the time that the little darling was a ferret, she would never have touched her. By the time she had identified her, she had found the jill to be a gentle creature totally without malice, had grown quite fond of her and was reluctant to give her back. I did offer her a youngster, but she didn't really have suitable quarters. Being a member of the cuddly-bunny-loving set she did not want to hear about the working ability of the little jill, but she always asks after *her* ferret when we meet.

I have been lucky enough always to manage to retrieve my escapees, but undoubtedly ferrets can and do cause problems if they get out. There is nothing worse than being confronted by an angry animal-owner who has your ferret and several dead chickens, pigeons or tame rabbits— you would feel just as upset in his place. The dear departed are always dear and usually rare and valuable examples of their breed. It is therefore commonsense to ensure that your pens are secure, for the sake of your pocket as well as your stock and your local reputation.

There are many different ways of accommodating ferrets; these range from the hutch to the ferret court, with several inbetween. The size and type of accommodation you choose will vary according to your means and circumstances, but you should aim for a minimum cage size of four feet in length and two feet in depth. This will house two ferrets in reasonable comfort; if you have the room or the pocket to allow for something larger, so much the better.

THE FERRET COURT

The ferret court was the method used by the warreners of old and is a superb way to house ferrets. It consists of a brick- or stone-walled enclosure divided into a run and separate sleeping quarters. In such spacious surroundings the ferrets can take as much exercise as they need to keep fit and healthy. I do not have the space for such splendid quarters, but I do have a pen in the garden equipped with a false burrow which has several entrances and exits. I put my ferrets in there on sunny days and watch them rush around, playing games and staging mock battles. Apart from valuable exercise, it also gives them the chance to view me from ground level and get used to my feet, something I consider particularly important with young stock. The first time I step in among them they usually rush down the nearest hole, but it does not take long for them to gain their confidence, which is one less hurdle to cross when they are put to work. The more room you can give them, the better they will be for it. Given space to live they are less likely to foul their food with their own droppings as can happen in confined quarters.

Some ferret-keepers house their stock on the community system in a shed or barn. While I approve of and adopt this method during the winter, when a group of ferrets will sleep together in a tangled heap and keep each other warm, I prefer to keep my breeding jills separate from each other come the spring, as this gives me more control over them. Apart from this time it is a good idea to house two animals together, for they do like company.

CAGES

Most people keep their stock in cages which are rather similar to the standard rabbit hutch and very easy to

44

construct, as they are just a simple box cage with an enclosed section at one end for sleeping quarters and a wire-mesh door. There is an alternative type in which the entire top opens, being hinged at the back; it was always known as a "cub" and is very useful, indeed preferable, for a single free-standing arrangement. It has the advantage of containing your ferrets while the door is open. Youngsters in particular are prone to fall out when a front-opening door is used, and once you have spent time juggling a litter of hungry kits back through such a door, you will appreciate the value of access from above. The only thing you have to guard against with the cub is trapping ferrets when you close the lid. This can be overcome by the use of a turned-over top edge which will act as a baffle.

Whether you choose a top- or front-opening type of cage, make it from close-boarded or tongued-and-grooved timber; the finished cage must be draft-free. Draft is a killer with most livestock, and if coupled with damp it will see your ferrets off very fast, for they are extremely susceptible to colds, chills and respiratory ills. To avoid drafts and protect the wood (not to mention the ferrets) from rain damage, you should cover the top and sides of outdoor cages with a layer of roofing felt. Never use corrugated iron as this acts like a cooker on hot days and causes condensation and dampness on cold ones. Aluminum sheet will act as a reflector in hot weather, even if the surface is dull, and for this reason is used for housing in the Middle East; nevertheless, it is just as bad a condenser on a damp day and should also be avoided. The roof should overhang the cage at the front and back to allow the water to drip clear. A reasonable overhang at the front will also keep off the worst of the weather while allowing a good flow of air. As long as you provide a dry sleeping section with plenty of bedding, you should never need to cover the cage front, even in the worst weather. Never fall into the trap of putting a piece of sacking over the front of the cage in wet weather; it retains the damp and is asking for trouble. A friend of mine once lost a perfectly healthy litter and their mother as a result of covering their cage with a sack during a thunderstorm and then forgetting to remove it afterward.

Another type of cage popular in some quarters is the one favored by mink-breeders. This is an all-wire construction with an enclosed wooden sleeping box at one end. Although it is very easy to clean, it seems rather spartan and chilling. This is fine for the mink-breeder, who needs to encourage his animals to put on a really dense coat and who also needs a cage which can be quickly made-up on a jig for easy construction, but it is not what I would choose for ferrets. I favor a wooden floor covered with a good layer of clean sawdust and plenty of hay and straw for bedding. With my methods I have never had any problems associated with damp, cold or filth.

If you are making a single unit, it is better to have it standing on strong legs at a sensible height from the ground. There are several reasons for this, not the least being that it will save your back. What is more important is that it will allow a free flow of air around the cage, which will, among other things, keep the timber in better condition. It will also allow you, if you wish, to drill a number of holes in the floor in the corner farthest from the sleeping quarters and cover them with a strong wire mesh to give your animal(s) a self-cleaning dung corner. This, however, is not practical if your cages are built on the tier system, as mine are, unless you allow for a false floor with a cleaning tray fitted underneath.

Having built good, draft-free, damp-proof and easily cleaned cages, you should, if you have not already done so, give some thought to the best place to position them. In spite of old stories to the contrary, ferrets should not be kept in the dark. They enjoy daylight and if kept outside have the chance to watch the passing scene. Ferrets are great watchers. Although they do not have very good long-distance sight, their glittering eyes do not miss much, and, of course, they use their ears and noses. However, it is not a good idea to place them in full and unrelenting sunshine for they will quickly overheat and collapse. It is better to pick a shady spot out of the prevailing wind and rain. Those of my ferrets who do live outside are shaded by a large hazel tree which filters both the sun and the wind yet is not close enough to drip on the cages and cause the fatal damp conditions. Whatever you provide in the way of accommodation for your ferrets, keep it clean and you are halfway there.

CHAPTER THREE   To Satisfy the Inner Ferret—Feeding

Ferrets fare best on a diet of fresh meat, preferably whole carcasses. Wild polecats are amazingly catholic in their choice of food, and an analysis of their stomach contents, coupled with observations of animals in the wild state, has shown that their diet, in addition to rabbits and other small mammals, extends to soft fruit, molluscs, fish, birds' eggs and, if the occasion presents itself, the birds themselves. Not for nothing is their French name the "hen cat." They seem prepared to try anything once and, like their larger relative the badger, can be classed as omnivorous opportunists. I have frequently come across the story about polecats catching frogs and storing them for a rainy day, alive but paralyzed, having bitten into the locomotive area of the frog's brain. It comes up often enough to make one suspect that it has a grain of truth, but I have yet to find any direct evidence of such reasoned and controlled behavior. Ferrets can be quite bright—and polecats are very bright—but I doubt whether they are quite so strong on forward planning. Once when my garden was full of frogs I watched the way in which my animals dealt with them. They came across the frogs in long grass and under shrubs, and, depending on how hungry they were, they either killed and ate them or totally ignored them. It was interesting to note that toads were left alone. I never found any "lobotomized" frogs, but maybe my ferrets are clever enough to know that their next meal is assured.

Clean, fresh water should always be available—even if it means serving it in your favorite mug!

Examination of the ferret's large intestine shows that it consists only of colon and rectum and is therefore not really suited for a high-fiber diet; with such an arrangement the fiber digestion must be negligible. This points to the need for a diet high in protein, such as meat, with the trace elements being made up from the gut contents of the "prey" species. In other words, not bread and milk or porridge, but whole-carcass meat.

Fed regularly on a diet of whole-carcass meat, ferrets will show their approval by their condition, being sleek, fit and shining with health. Depending on the size of the offering, they will eat bones, fur, feathers and all. Their only other requirement will be fresh water; this is particularly important and must be readily available at all times, as blood-meals create a real thirst.

You must temper my advice regarding whole-carcasses with common sense and tailor the size of the meal to the appetite of the animal. It is no earthly use, and it defeats the object of good husbandry, to throw a huge rabbit or a whole hen in with one tiny jill and then leave her with it for several days. I remember that when I bought my first jill ferret, she was caged on her own with a none-too-fresh calf's head. You will find that, as with other animals, appetite varies considerably—and of course the ferrets themselves vary greatly in size, from tiny eight-ounce jills to huge hobs weighing over four pounds—so there is no way that they will eat the same amount. However, as a general guide, I find that a large hob caged with a jill will eat a whole gray squirrel at one sitting—squirrels feature frequently on their menu. One pair I have will eat the lot except for the pelt and maybe the claws, while another will eat everything.

USING ROAD CASUALTIES

Road casualties in the form of rabbits, squirrels, small birds and the odd pheasant or two can make up a considerable proportion of your ferrets' diet. It is essential that you rise early to search for these or your gleanings will be either very high or very flat! It has often been put about by my non-ferreting friends that I can be seen hovering over country lanes on summer mornings, giving a passable imitation of a vulture. Along with many men of my age who shoot a bit, I suffer from a small loss of hearing in the upper registers (in my case the left side). I always jokingly put it down to the shriek of disapproval from my wife when I stop on the way home from a late night out at some dressy affair to pick up the bloody corpse of some unfortunate rabbit or bird!

This method of providing meat for your ferrets is only profitable if you live in an area well-populated with wildlife. A large town is unlikely to provide a regular supply of usable bodies—a fair number of cats and feral pigeons are killed each week, but not enough to make the effort of finding them worthwhile. Feral pigeons are used by many as a diet. Indeed, I have heard of one or two ferret-owning policemen who shoot roosting pigeons under railway arches and bridges while on night duty. I would not advise anyone else to try it—imagine trying to explain it away to the desk sergeant!

Apart from the effort involved, there are other considerations to be taken into account when collecting roadside casualties. Rats, cats, foxes and pigeons—all readily accepted by ferrets—should, in my opinion, be left alone by even the most vulturine ferret-keeper. Most of these creatures are very aware of traffic, so it is more than likely that those that do get killed, particularly in urban areas, are already doomed by some deadly disease or poison which they can posthumously pass on to your stock. In addition, many urban foxes suffer from mange, which you can yourself pick up, via your ferrets, in fairly short order. As one who has suffered from this highly infectious sarcoptic mange—in humans it is referred to as scabies—I can tell you that it is unpleasant, uncomfortable and difficult and expensive to get rid of.

51

Make sure that road casualties are both clean and fresh. Do not feed decomposing carcasses as there is a risk of food poisoning from a variety of nasty bacteria; do not feed any carcass without opening it and checking its condition, even items you have shot yourself—tapeworms and liver-flukes are things a ferret is better off without. If you feed pigeons to your ferrets it is worth checking for avian tuberculosis, which shows up as white nodules on the liver and intestines. This disease is quite common in pigeons, and a good guide can be obtained from the plumage, which tends to be darker in affected birds. Any suspect corpse must be burned. (If you eat pigeon yourself this is a point worth watching.)

The number of days that I can go out and shoot or trap something for my ferrets is fairly limited. I did once make a sparrow-trap though. This was placed on the roof of my shed where I had been feeding birds for several months, and I baited it up in the approved manner for some time before I closed it. On the first morning after it had been set I found three birds sitting inside, two hedge sparrows and a cock house sparrow. The hedge sparrows are not sparrows at all, but accentors, song birds on the British protected list, and therefore had to be released. In any case, I like to see them about, with their quiet confiding ways as they follow each other around the garden. This left me with one lonely, frightened cock sparrow. I hadn't the heart to kill him, and anyway, what use was one sparrow shared with twenty-plus ferrets? I let him go, too. Those three must have gone off and warned all their friends, as I never had another sparrow in that trap.

If you decide to build a bird-trap, whether it be a sparrow-trap in your garden or a crow-trap in the woods, you *must* check it every day, preferably more than once. Song birds and protected species *must* be released, no matter how much you need something with which to feed your stock. If you are going to trap, *do it right or don't do it at all.* Ferrets and ferreters have had a bad enough press over the years without anyone adding to it by breaking the law and by causing unnecessary suffering.

NON-MEAT FOODS

Although basically a carnivore, the ferret is able to do well on other diets. The best-known and most frequently used alternative is bread and milk. Ferrets like it and have been known to live long and full lives on nothing else, but probably they did so in spite of, rather than because of, such a boring and inadequate diet. Bread-and-milk slop produces loose and unpleasant droppings, particularly when fed with an addition of margarine. One of the problems of such a diet is a build-up of tartar on the surface of the teeth and gums; this can be overcome by the addition of small amounts of bone. For this reason you should never give a totally boneless meat diet. There are occasions when I *would* sanction the feeding of bread-and-milk slop. It does no harm, rather the reverse, to give warm milk with bread or egg as a supplement when rearing youngsters or as a tummy-warmer on cold mornings, but I would never use it as a full diet.

Most people keep relatively small numbers of ferrets, usually fewer than ten adult animals. In contrast, as I have already mentioned, ferret colonies in research laboratories can run into several thousand animals in a single unit. This conjures up a delightful picture of dozens of laboratory technicians whizzing around the countryside collecting dead rabbits! In fact, laboratory ferrets are usually fed on pellet foods or on a commercial powdered diet intended for mink. The latter is fed as a mash and is very successful, particularly with jills rearing litters. In the *UFAW Manual of Laboratory Animals,* Hammond and Chesterman mention that they have successfully used a commercially available pellet food originally intended for weaning pigs. They report that over a period of ten years they reared something in the order of 1,000 ferrets. Preference was given to diets which were not supplemented by copper, which is frequently added to pig diets as a growth promoter. In view of the fact that most ferret-breeders are striving to breed smaller animals, this is an important point to remember.

There are now quite a number of dry pellet foods available for dogs and cats which are also suitable for ferrets. The one I find best is made by Purina; I have found it is accepted sufficiently readily by my own ferrets to be kept as an emergency standby. I would not recommend the use of the crushed maize/oats/meatmeal type of dog food because of the high fiber content. Purina and other similar pellet foods contain a higher proportion of dried meat and, if moistened with hot water, will give off the unmistakable smell of paunch (stomach); this is a great favorite with dogs, as most breeders will know—it is invariably taken before anything else that is on offer. Therefore, when going over from a fresh meat diet to one of dry pellets, it is a good idea to moisten the pellets to bring out the smell and encourage your animals to feed rather than turn their backs in disgust. If you decide to add a strange food to the diet of any animal, you may expect the animal to be slow to take to it unless encouraged; ferrets are no different and can be very stubborn about strange foods other than meat. When dry foods first came on the market there were a great many cases of renal atrophy in cats which were denied access to sufficient water. The same *could* happen to ferrets, though I have never heard of a case, so beware.

Pellet foods have much to recommend them when used properly: they are well-balanced, clean and hygienic; they do not go bad; they can be stored without the use of expensive freezer space; and they do not encourage flies in the dung corner. I sometimes feel that for pure ease and freedom from the problems of meat diets I ought to go over to an all-pellet diet and have done with it. Breeders of show and meat rabbits have been feeding their stock entirely on pellets for years now and do not have to scour the hedgerows for dandelions and plantains as I did when I used to help my father feed his stud of over a hundred top-class show rabbits. But however I look at it, from the ferret's angle it must be a rather boring diet. As an alternative to the dry pellets, you might try canned dog food or the moist pellets. These will be accepted by most ferrets but are a rather expensive method of feeding unless your numbers are small; they also tend to make the ferrets scour (become diarrhetic) when they are first put onto them.

A BALANCED DIET

As you can see, there are a number of things which will delight your ferret's palate. Essentially, you have to try to feed a sensible, balanced diet based on raw meat in some form. Until very recently I fed my stock on a basic diet of chicken giblets supplemented by as much whole-carcass meat as I could get. I have now changed their mainstay to culled day-old chicks from the hatcheries. These, together with the very varied types of whole-carcasses (including rabbits, squirrels, pigeons, etc.) as well as pellet foods and, at the appropriate times, some bread and milk, form a pretty varied menu.

The Ever-Increasing Horde—Breeding

Once you have provided your ferrets with suitable accommodations and overcome the initial problems of keeping them, you will be unusual if you do not have a yen to try breeding a few. There has always been a great deal of myth and legend surrounding ferrets, and most of the myths seem to relate to the problems associated with breeding and rearing. However, given a normal amount of luck, if you follow the advice in this book about sensible housing and feeding and the advice given in this chapter, you should find that ferrets are frequently rather easier to breed than they are to sell.

Ferrets come into breeding age and condition for the first time at around ten months old, in the spring following their birth. The breeding season starts in late March to early April, although it can be advanced or delayed by a number of factors, principally the weather. An early spring and the close proximity of hobs can bring the jills forward several weeks. I have heard of litters being produced in late February, but this unusually early arrival is more likely to be the result of a second estrus in the 12-month cycle.

THE HOBS (MALES)

Although seemingly fertile throughout the greater part of the year, the hob comes into full breeding condition earlier than the jill, at around the end of December. His testes, which are drawn up into the body out of season,

Runts are weak offspring that have been rejected by the mother. It is necessary to humanely destroy the runt if it is not doing well, unless it appears fit and active. If it is healthy enough to carry on, you will have to assist with hand-rearing, since the mother will not take it back once she has rejected it.

drop down into the scrotum again at around this time. If put into a strange place or within sight of jills, he will run around, chattering loudly and rubbing himself cat-like against any projecting surface, scent-marking for all he is worth. He smells rather stronger than before (his critics would not have believed this possible) and becomes belligerent with other hobs.

With the onset of the breeding season, it is not a good idea to cage two strange hobs together or even two hobs that haved lived together all their lives if you have had to separate them for any period longer than three or four days. Such action can lead to some terrible fights which may well end in the death of one or both of them. Quite recently I heard a sad story from a lady in the West Country. She was the proud owner of two large polecat/ ferret hobs which were kept as family pets. They were litter brothers and had never been separated; however, when they reached adulthood in their first spring they were not only starting to smell rather strongly but were also coming to blows. They were pretty evenly matched.

When the situation did not resolve itself, their fond owner, who thought the world of them, consulted her local vet. It was decided that the best thing would be to neuter them; after some discussion the operation was successfully carried out. (Castration is a good idea in such circumstances, as not only does it quiet the animals down, but it also reduces the smell of rampant hob ferret.) However, all was not well. The staff at the surgery made the mistake of placing the unconscious animals in the same cage to await recovery from the anesthetic. When they came round, the two hobs were, in their minds at least, still full males, in strange surroundings, with strange smells about them and their companion's familiar smells masked by disinfectants, etc.; on top of this they were in some pain. The fight which followed left two dead ferrets, one very unhappy lady and one embarrassed vet.

Provided they are not separated, two hobs will live together fairly happily throughout their entire lives. They establish a pecking order (frequently homosexual). One is always the boss and the other recognizes that fact. However, it is a fragile relationship, and if it is disturbed all hell will break loose. Consequently, I never house two hobs together after the middle of January—if at all.

THE JILLS (FEMALES)

Fortunately, no such problems beset jills; under normal circumstances they can be kept together throughout the year without any trouble. Total strangers will mix readily, even at the height of the breeding season. Now and again you do come across the odd jill who is aggressive, but if you run her in with a group for short periods at a time, she usually settles down. I house my jills in pairs unless I intend to breed from them, in which case I give them individual quarters.

Once a jill comes into breeding condition she will stay that way, unless mated, for several months (usually until the middle of August). The condition which is known as being in heat or, more correctly, estrus is shown by the enlargement of the vaginal opening from a tiny, insignificant slit to a swollen pink vulva approaching the size of a small hazelnut. It is not uncommon for unmated jills to go out of estrus after a short time and into a phantom pregnancy. Some even produce milk and will, if given the chance, rear orphan kits or, if housed with a nursing jill, will assist with the upbringing of the family. More often, though, the jill will stay in heat unless mated. For generations ferret-breeders have believed that unless you allow a jill to have a litter by her second season she will sicken and die. It is true that a number of unmated jills do die each year, but I don't know of anyone who has taken a jill for a post-mortem examination and been told: "Your jill died because she was not bred from!" The various causes of medical problems with jills are examined in the last chapter; for the moment, I will say only that females who are never bred from and females who are regularly bred from stand less chance of suffering from womb infections than those who are only occasionally bred from. Provided they are kept in good condition, unmated jills will have few problems; they do tend to lose weight, but with normal care that can soon be rectified. I have several maiden jills whose ages range from 18 months to five years. They are all fit and well, never having had a day's illness in their lives; added to this is the fact that, contrary to another myth, they are very keen workers.

The reason a jill ferret stays in heat and receptive to males for long periods is that, in common with several other animals including the domestic cat, the breeding cycle is governed by a system known as induced ovulation—the eggs are not released into the womb for fertilization until mating has taken place. There are several ways of controlling estrus in ferrets. The most recent method is by the injection of a hormone suppressant, but it is rather expensive. The simplest and cheapest way at present is to use a suppressant in tablet form, such as Ovarid, which you can obtain from your vet. This, in effect, puts your jill "on the pill" for the normal period of her season. Tiny doses given daily will suppress the heat, but they must be kept up. One pill is enough for three jills over four days; quartered and crushed it can be fed disguised in the food or given with a drop of milk, making sure that each jill not only gets her share, but also that she does actually take it. The pill does not dissolve very easily and if left in the bottom of the bowl will be ignored. The man who first told me of this method discovered that the jill will spit out any pill, and he encourages his by giving it in chocolate, which they like. I have only tried this for one season, but it does work. Although the dosage seems small, both my local vet and I feel that it is still a little high, so if I try it again I intend to reduce it slightly and see what happens. A note of caution is in place here, as all hormone treatment is suspect today and it is just possible that the cure could become a killer. Hormone treatments have been known to cause cancer of the womb. Even with the large number of jills I keep, I still feel that to leave them to it is much the safest course.

SELECTING FOR BREEDING

You should select only the best ferrets for breeding: not just those who work well, but those that are both physically and mentally fit as well, for often a good and clever worker may have some physical defect which you should not pass on. This rule applies to all livestock but is often forgotten when it comes to ferrets. There are plenty of good ferrets around, so there is no need to breed from weak, diseased, neurotic or inbred stock. Keep your bloodlines fresh, for inbreeding, unless carefully controlled by someone with a knowledge of genetics, rarely brings out the best, and all too often it brings out the worst.

Never be tempted to breed from your ferrets in the hope

of making a profit. Over the past two years, well-reared, clean and healthy young ferrets have been sold at Guildford Market for as little as 5p (about 10¢) each. A friend of mine who sold some 20 lovely young kits at this price did not bother to collect his check from the auctioneer. Although at the time he was relieved to be rid of them, for they were eating him out of house and home, he ruefully told me afterward that the box cost him more than he got for the ferrets!

In order to ensure that your selected ferrets are worth breeding from, it is advisable to wait until their second season. Apart from giving them time to reach full maturity, it will also enable you to get to know their value. These comments apply equally to both sexes, but to illustrate the point let me tell you about a polecat/ferret jill I bought as an eight-week-old kit. She was a little darling, a great favorite with the family and a very attractive animal. She loved a game and was a pleasure to handle. I had put her through all the normal working-up processes, and, although I hadn't used her too often in the first winter, she was a good bolter. In her second winter she changed completely; she was still perfect at home, but once she went into a rabbit hole she would emerge spitting and biting like a mad thing. The first time it happened I came to the conclusion that she had come across something which had really frightened her. But from then on, every time she was entered to rabbit she did the same thing, fairly screaming with rage. I finally came to the conclusion that, whatever the cause, she was a nut-case and of no use to me either as a worker or a breeding jill. Sad to say, she had to go.

MATING

Once you have the right animals you are ready to begin. Having recognized that the jill is ready to be mated and allowed for the fact that you will soon have to find extra accommodations for your increasing stock, you should

Handling your ferrets often while they are still young will help to make them more docile and affectionate pets. It is important for them to get used to you (your hands, your voice, your scent) and for you to get used to them in order to establish a mutual trust. You can begin to handle the kits when they are approximately two weeks old.

go ahead and introduce your jill to the hob (assuming that she is not already living with him). Most of the hobs I have come across do not bother about such fine points, but if you take her to him rather than the other way round, then he will not have to overcome the territorial defense attitude which the jill may put up. Provided both animals are in good condition there will be no time wasted; after a few moments of mutual sniffing and low excited chattering, the hob will grab the jill by the scruff of her neck and haul her, protesting loudly, off to bed, where they should be left in peace. In spite of the ensuing noises, the jill will generally suffer no damage apart from a little swelling around the neck and a few bite marks. It is thought by some that the neck-biting may be a trigger for ovulation and that unmarked jills will not be fertilized. However, I have noticed that hobs who are allowed several jills in any one season often do not mark them at all, yet the jills still become pregnant.

Mating can be completed in half an hour or less (I once had a hob mate a jill in under five minutes when two animals were put together in error, and she produced a litter of ten), but I prefer the pair to be together for 24 hours. By this time the hob should have released the jill from his hold and they should both be pacing the cage ready for their next meal. Afterward the jill should be returned to her own quarters. I prefer to keep the sexes apart until I am ready to mate them; in this way I know just when the kits are due and can make suitable arrangements. The less hit-and-miss you are about the whole thing, the better the chances of success. You can, of course, leave the pair together, provided that your cage is big enough and provided that you trust you hob not to eat his offspring. He is less likely to do so if there is plenty of space and if he has an alternative place to sleep. Generally, if you get them through the first week he is unlikely to do so.

As an exception to my own rule, I do keep one pair together on a permanent basis, for the fun of it and to prove that it can be done. They live in an eight-foot by three foot earth-floored, underwired pen in which I have placed a couple of large logs and a small pile of rocks. What with these and the chance to dig holes all the time, they are very fit and the hob has plenty to occupy him. A huge and gentle creature, he takes his turn in looking after his family when they arrive, and although he is a bit heavy-handed with the discipline once they are weaned, he is a model father.

After mating has taken place under the more normal controlled conditions, you can expect the litter to arrive in six weeks. It is usually on time, very often right to the day, but do not worry if the jill is a few days overdue as some do go on into the seventh week. At least by controlling the mating you will know when the litter *should* have arrived if a vet ever needs to know.

If the mating was successful, the jill's vulva will return to its normal size after a few days. If this does not happen then it is probable that the hob was not successful in his attempt to couple with her, and another attempt should be made. In my experience this rarely happens; more often, mating takes place and in spite of all the normal signs no litter is produced. There are two possible reasons for this: either the jill has had a phantom pregnancy or she has eaten the litter. The sudden reduction of her size plus very dark feces in the dung corner indicate the latter; in a phantom pregnancy the signs reduce over a much longer period. Infanticidal behavior is more likely to occur in young jills with their first litter, although in many cases it is thought to be caused by a hormone imbalance. In such cases the jill invariably comes straight back into season and if remated will probably rear the subsequent litter without any trouble.

PREGNANCY

During the first two weeks of your jill's pregnancy you should make doubly sure that she is free from parasites. I do this automatically before I mate the jills, including worming them with a reduced dose of a cat or dog wormer, but I also check again for external parasites in the early stages. Having made sure that your breeding stock is clean, it makes sense to do the same for their quarters. When the litter arrives you will not be able to clean the nest area for several weeks; this will give any parasites the chance to build up their numbers undisturbed, so do try to start off with clean quarters.

Ferrets are not fragile little flowers; they are well able to look after themselves and sometimes resent too much molly-coddling and fuss during pregnancy and rearing, but it is wise to keep an eye on things generally. Diet and exercise are two of the things over which you have control, so make sure that your jill is well-fed and able to take some exercise. Do not, however, overfeed her—you want her fit, not fat. Rather than increase her ration on the principle that she is eating for her unborn family as well as herself, you should cut her rations slightly as her time approaches. She will put on unwanted fat if allowed to overfeed as she will naturally be less athletic toward the end of her pregnancy. About a week before the litter is due, I start to give on a daily basis a little warmed milk with some powdered calcium added; this guards against calcium loss during the rearing of the kits. I hear of many cases of jills fed on low-calcium diets suffering badly from milk fever when rearing large litters. I receive regular requests for help and advice on this point every year, and the remedy is simple. The cost of a can of calcium supplement is small compared with vet fees should the problem occur. Once a jill has reached the stage of suffering from milk fever she can only be saved by the injection of large doses of calcium.

During the final week of pregnancy, give the cage one last good cleaning and make sure the nest area is well-supplied with clean hay or straw. Once this is done you can leave the jill alone to settle down and get on with things, for she is well able to deal with the delivery herself. I recently met a doctor from Sussex who likes to attend the delivery of his kits. He is in that respect well qualified but must rate as unusual. He tends to think of and talk about his ferrets as though they are people, and he certainly has a rapport with them. Like me, he believes in getting to know them right from the start.

One thing which breeders often find alarming in their first season is the way that the expectant jills go into a sudden and dramatic molt, throwing off their long winter coats. If you are not aware of what is happening, you may think your jill is suffering from some dreadful skin disorder in spite of your previous efforts to ensure that she was clean. Do not worry about it, for it is often the first sign of the forthcoming family. The fur quite literally comes out in handfuls, leaving a short close coat which shows up her outline, making her condition obvious.

A while ago my intrepid escape-artist, the polecat/ferret jill, was mated to an untried hob. Apart from the fact that she went out of estrus within a very few days, she exhibited no further signs of pregnancy and was as slim as ever under her thick coat. My wife and I discussed her at length—was she or wasn't she? We were not at all sure. Then quite suddenly, and rather later than I had previously experienced, off came her winter coat. "That's it," I told my wife. "She's there. But I'll be surprised if she has more than two or three kits, for she's as slim as a rake." Just to confound me she produced ten with bones like foxhounds, the strongest litter I had seen for years. Goodness knows where she put them, as she never showed at all right up to the last.

A litter of eight healthy kits at two and a half weeks old. They are able to move about even though their eyes are not yet open. These are polecat/ferrets, as evidenced by their dark color.

THE NEW LITTER

When the litter does arrive you will be left in no doubt, for apart from the obvious slimming down of the mother you will also be able to hear the squeaking of the newborn kits. They are born blind, furless and totally helpless, with pink bodies and blunt little faces, their eyes tightly shut and difficult to spot. Polecat or white, they are all the same at this stage and it is some days before any differences begin to appear. Before the fur begins to grow and the polecat kits take on a darker appearance, the eye line will begin to show as a dark line even though the actual bulge of the closed eye is not yet obvious. Each kit weighs around ½-¾ ounces and is around one inch long, just like a little wriggling grub with a tiny tail. To start with they are very vocal, but after a few days they settle down into a quieter routine of feeding and sleeping.

We now come to the question of whether or not we should look into the nest. There is an old belief, still very strong, that you should not interfere with the jill and her litter in any way until the kits leave the nest and begin to feed themselves. However, I feel that provided you know your jills and they know and *trust* you, which should be the case by the time they are due to deliver, you are unlikely to upset them by looking. But do not charge in like a bull in a china shop—wait for the right moment. The best chances are at normal feeding times. If your kits have arrived in the middle of the night or in the early hours of the morning, you will hear them when you go to give the jill her morning drop of milk. By this time she will have come to expect a drink and will almost certainly leave her babies to come out for it when she hears you approach. If she does not appear and you can hear noises which indicate the arrival of the family, leave her until later as she may still be in labor. I would recommend that, when inspecting a litter of small kits, you make a point of giving the jill a drink. Apart from being welcome to her, this also means that she has to stay with the bowl while you are looking rather than running back and forth with lumps of food. In this way you can check with the minimum of disturbance.

If the nest has been covered over, however, I leave it alone for a day or two. I do not go out of my way to upset my nursing jill, as even the tamest can become a tiger at this time. Make your approaches with care and you will soon find what her reaction is going to be. Do not rub your hands in the dung corner before looking at the family as some rabbit breeders still recommend! If you have handled your ferrets properly from the beginning and not just thrown food in from a distance at irregular intervals, all your stock will be used to your scent and know it presents no threat.

Your first view of the kits should be a quick one; there is no need to try and handle them unless the jill has done something stupid, like delivering them outside the nest in the cold. Just check to see that all is well and try to get some idea of the number so that you will know if the litter is reduced at any stage in the rearing. The average litter is around seven, my own average is ten and the largest litter known to me, all reared, is 19. The sex ratio is about equal, in my own case exactly so. (It is strange that, to date, the litter numbers of captive-bred wild polecats seem to be much smaller, with a bias toward males of around four to one. However, my figures are at present taken from a small sample and as the sample size increases the ratio will, I am sure, balance out.)

After this first swift look, leave the family alone until the next morning when you can have a closer look at the jill. She may resent handling, but if you have gotten to know her well she should allow you to handle her long enough to check that she is clean and not covered in blood from a difficult labor, is supple and active and is producing milk. In spite of all the previous handling and familiarization, some mothers do turn nasty, so you have to look out for your fingers. The jills can give the impression that they are prepared to take your arm off at the knee! I cannot put too much stress on the point that you should know all your ferrets very well and have their complete trust. If this *is* the case, you will have a calm, unruffled mother whose normal state is known to you, and you will be quicker to spot any abnormal behavior. Most times the jill should remain fairly tranquil. I have heard of jills drawing their owner's hands into the nest and allowing the kits to be handled when only a few days old. This has happened to me just once—the jill took my thumb and pulled it into the nest. I would like to believe that she was showing me how much she trusted me, but it is more likely that the short-sighted animal mistook my thumb for one of her kits, which were about the same size.

Provided my nursing jills do not become distressed by my presence, I continue to check the progress of the litter every three or four days for the first two weeks, always at feeding times when the mother is otherwise occupied. When comparing my methods with those of others, it is perhaps relevant that my nursing jills are kept in a shed in a quiet corner and therefore live a quiet life with no sudden happenings—such as a cat jumping on the top of their cages—or large fluctuations in temperature. Because I have always made regular checks on the growing litter, I have come to know just what stage the kits have reached at any given time and can make qualified judgments on their progress. After two weeks I check them and handle some almost every day. They get to know my hand and voice, and we seem to establish some sort of rapport. However, if I am really honest with myself, I have to admit that it often does not make the slightest difference, as the first thing they do when they open their eyes is bite me. Without exception, young ferrets will treat anything put near their mouths as food until they learn better.

I continue to give my jills their daily ration of milk right through the rearing time. As the youngsters start to leave the nest for their first ventures into the outside world, I begin to include a little bread or dry-pellet food with the milk. As already stated, I am not an advocate of bread and milk as a steady diet, but it is a useful supplement to the main diet of meat. If you are lucky enough to have access to sufficient fresh meat, so much the better, for if you have 30 or 40 growing youngsters, food supplies can be a considerable worry. I add a raw egg to the bread and milk every day or so at the rate of one egg to every five young ferrets.

It has been said that young ferrets do not open their eyes or attempt to leave the nest until they are six weeks old, but this has never been my experience. Mine are invariably out and about for short periods at the beginning of their fourth week with one eye open; strong on their legs and reasonably self-supporting at five weeks; and like a bowl of piranha fish at six weeks. From four to six weeks they are, in my opinion, at their most attractive. Given the time, I will spend hours with them, for this is the period when I decide which ones I am going to keep. Those I pick are singled out for special attention: they get fussed over, tickled, carried around in my pocket, introduced to the rest of the family and generally made to feel at home. I believe you cannot start too soon with the business of getting to know your ferret. As for the rest, they still get their share of attention but on a group basis rather than as individuals. Handling a group of young kits can be very difficult, particularly with a large litter and especially at feeding time, when the element of competition for the choicest morsels makes you doubt your sanity, for in spite of the fact that they do not have any real strength they can still hang on to your fingers. A painless way of steadying young ferrets is to wait until they have eaten their fill and are a little sleepy before handling them;

In the event your jill dies and you must hand-rear the young, it is best to feed them every two hours with about half a teaspoon of warm milk for each kit. Milk can be prepared by mixing a rearing

powder with water and offering it in an eyedropper as shown here. It is wise to consult a veterinarian, especially if the kits are under three weeks of age.

that is unless you have hands like a chief stoker's, in which case they will soon learn that they are wasting their time. At eight weeks, however, well-grown ferrets are capable of drawing blood, and that is not something I encourage. The idea is to teach them that my hands *bring* food, rather than leave them with the idea that they *are* food.

One of the problems associated with keeping ferrets is that of flies. Because ferrets are fed on meat, they attract large numbers of flies in the summer. Under normal conditions these do not appear to worry the ferrets, but problems arise with youngsters in the nest. You cannot change the bedding until their eyes are open, as this kind of disturbance is more than most jills will tolerate. Flies will lay their eggs in the corner where the jill places her food, and, regardless of how careful you are to make sure that no food is left after every meal, the flies will still be attracted by the blood and the smell. Even if you tie large pieces of meat to the bars of the cage to stop the jill from carrying food into the nest, she will still contrive to do so, and in a few days the nest will be crawling with maggots. I therefore try to keep that corner clean. I have fly-screens over the windows and door of my ferret shed in an attempt to reduce the problem, but some flies always manage to get in. Consequently, once in the shed they have to contend with the fumes from a solid-chemical fly-killer or a burst from an aerosol spray. The manufacturers assure me that the small-room version of the solid-chemical type is quite safe, provided you do not hang it directly over the food of the ferrets. In some areas the old-fashioned sticky fly-papers are available again; however, I do find that not only are they rather messy, but they are also less effective.

The sooner you can get the youngsters away from their mother, the sooner you can get back to a normal cleaning routine. Once my litters have reached seven weeks I separate them from the jill, and at eight weeks I split them into smaller groups, by which time they are ready to be sold (if I am lucky) or given away. I break up the litters once they are weaned, basically for reasons of cleanliness—only those who have kept ten or more ferrets in one cage can appreciate just how mucky that cage can get in 12 hours.

IS HAND-REARING POSSIBLE?

If you follow the methods described for feeding and breeding, you should normally have no trouble producing sound and healthy young ferrets. However, even the best breeders can produce the occasional runt. If this happens, be totally ruthless and destroy the weaklings right away. By this I do not mean destroy a ferret kit just because it is smaller than their rest of its siblings. So long as it is fit and active and not suffering from a permanently swollen belly it should be allowed to carry on. It is the obvious weaklings and "poor doers" that one must watch out for. Outside the normal situations, there are a number of things which can cause death while the kits are in the nest or when they are being weaned off, but I will deal with these at a later stage.

Meanwhile, what do you do if the mother of a litter becomes sick and dies with tiny babies in the nest? With luck it will never happen to you, but just in case, you ought to be prepared. Jill ferrets, like any other creatures, do sometimes have trouble giving birth. More often than not the problem does not show right away, and by the time you realize that something is wrong, it is too late to save the jill. If this happens you will be faced with a considerable problem, the solution of which will depend on how keen you are to save the kits, how old they are and even how many of you there are in your family.

The age of the kits will frequently determine whether or not you can attempt to rear them. If they are over three weeks they will have already started to take some solid food and you will have no real trouble. The difficult ones are those under two weeks. The amount of attention they will need is such that if you have a large litter and do not have a family prepared to assist, it is not worth trying, for you will inevitably lose them. Of course, if you have another jill with a litter of a similar age the problem is greatly reduced. Nursing jills will normally accept other youngsters without fuss, but do not overload them. It must be obvious that if you have a jill rearing eight or ten kits of her own, she cannot be expected to rear another eight or ten as well. Large litters do pull a jill down very much, and it is sometimes wiser to cull your litter anyway. Many breeders automatically cull their litter down to around five to take the load off the jill and reduce their own problems when it comes to selling off their surplus stock at the end of the rearing time. I do not cull my litter, preferring to feed my stock well and then have the choice of the whole litter. However, with jills producing anything up to 19 kits, committing yourself to hand-rearing can be an enormous problem, for once committed it becomes something of a point of honor not to lose any.

Some five years ago I was faced with this problem. As a result, I learned a lot more about young ferrets and was left with a much greater admiration for my nursing jills. One of my favorite jills died after producing a litter of ten. She appeared a little below par on the second day following the birth, and, in spite of strenuous attempts to save her, she died on the fourth day. Her kits were starving—when I found her dead they were crawling about the cage in a desperate search for sustenance. I gathered them up, took them to the house and, after a rapid discussion, my wife and I set about the task of trying to save them. The first thing was to get them warm or they would have died of cold. Their insistent squeaks for food had taken on a slow rasping sound from which I deduced they were on their last legs. We put them in an empty one-gallon ice cream container with a piece of blanket folded on the bottom and put that near the stove. This was a mistake;

on the second day one of the stronger ones managed to get between the folds of the blanket and died of suffocation. After that I put them in a single-ferret traveling box filled with soft hay, and we had no further trouble of that kind.

Having warmed them up, we set about trying to feed them. Most of the milk seemed to go outside rather than inside to start with, as we were using a cotton swab soaked in milk. Neither my wife nor I had tried to hand-rear any small mammal, let alone anything so tiny as these little mites. At four days old they were only about one and a half inches long and under one ounce in weight. They would not keep their heads still when we tried to feed them and were soon covered in milk. Another way had to be found. We ransacked the house looking for eye-droppers and fountain pen fillers, but they were all far too big for the tiny mouths. In the end we found a glass pipette in my daughter's scent-making kit. (Now most pet shops sell a puppy and kitten rearing set which includes some very small pipettes.) Once we had found the dropper, we had to teach the kits to drink the milk from it. I could not hold them at first, as they were so small that my fingers simply got in the way. My wife was able to hold them comfortably between finger and thumb when wrapped in a small piece of towel. The trick was in holding the tiny head still until they had located the source of the milk. (With the head bobbing about you feel that at any moment you are going to impale the infant on the feeder.) Once they had learned this lesson there was no looking back, and they were soon suckling happily. After that first feed they settled down to sleep for at least an hour. Flushed with success, we began to take stock of the situation. Just what should we give them to drink, how much and how often? We decided on a commercial pet-rearing powder, but we had no idea what strength to use. The maker could give no advice as they had never analyzed ferret's milk. All they could tell us was not to let it dry on

The kits (infants) should be weaned from their mother at approximately seven weeks. The two pictured here are seven weeks old and are ready to take care of themselves.

the faces of the kits or the hair would probably fall out and leave permanent bald patches.

By trial and error we settled the kits into a regular routine of two-hourly feedings, each consisting of about half a teaspoon of the milk. When you make up very small amounts of warm milk it quickly gets cold. We found that the answer was to make up the desired amount at blood heat and then float the small plastic bowl containing it in a larger bowl of hot water; in this way the temperature can be maintained for quite a long time. The formula needs to be rather stronger than the standard kitten puppy mix, but you must always take care: if you are too heavy-handed with the powder-to-water ratio you can upset the balance and end up with dead kits. The standard mix is one part powder to three parts water; we found that the best ratio was two parts powder to five parts water. This may not sound like much of a difference, but it increases the powder by 20%.

To set about feeding any number, it is necessary to work out a system and have all the equipment ready before you start. You will need a small bowl to hold the milk (plastic storage bowls are ideal), a larger bowl to hold the hot water for floating the food bowl, two other bowls of warm water, two clean cloths and a soft dry towel, plus of course the dropper—it is a good idea to have one or two spare droppers, for if you drop and break one in the middle of the night because you are only half-awake, you are in trouble.

The kits should be kept in a closed but ventilated box filled with soft hay. As they grow, assuming that they are very small when you start, you will need another box. With two boxes, you can transfer the kits that have been fed to a clean box, and so remove the possibility of confusion. Take the first kit from the box with as little fuss as possible—the object is to avoid waking the others. During the first two weeks of their lives they do not have the ability to evacuate their bowels without stimulation. Their mother does this by licking them. In the box and without their mother, they will, if awakened by light or sound, start to clamber around, squeaking for attention. The movement stimulates their bowels and they defecate all over each other! They soon become very smelly, very wet and very cold—the latter being the major cause for concern, as they can quickly chill, catch pneumonia and die. If you can get some of them fed before the others wake up, then you have a head start and do not have to bathe so many.

Once you have the first kit in your hand, wipe its bottom with a small piece of wet cloth to imitate the mother's licking and it will empty both bladder and bowel. Assuming that it is still clean and dry, you can then start to give it its feed. If it is not clean, you must bathe it carefully in one of the bowls of warm water and dry it properly with the soft towel. I find that they really enjoy this part, and when fed after a bath they will sleep like tops. (No matter how careful we were, the kits always woke up en-masse at least twice every day. We bathed them so often we began to think they might grow up to be otters!) You may be wondering why you need two bowls of warm water. The reason is that, while you are bathing a kit it may often empty its bowel again and, if you put it down while you make up a fresh bowl, it will get cold and impatient, yell its little head off and wake up the rest. Once the kit has been fed, wipe its face clean, stimulate it again, put it in the clean warm box and start on the next one. Remember this has to be done every two hours, day and night, for anything up to four weeks—hence my comment about the size and willingness of your own family, for you cannot do it alone; in the early stages, as soon as you have finished one feed it will be almost time to start again.

At three weeks of age you should cut the feedings down

to every three hours, and twice a day you can give tiny amounts of scraped meat on a spoon. Naturally, as the babies grow you should increase the amount of milk given at each feeding, taking care to satisfy but not overfill. It is all too easy to overfeed the kits (which distends the belly and turns them into little balloons) in an attempt to cut down the number of feedings. Do not, on any account, put meat into the nest for them to try, or you will be spending all your time cleaning them up; this can be a serious mistake. I did it once on the advice of a zoo and it nearly cost me the litter! The jill naturally takes food to her litter in the nest, but she is with them all the time. If left alone to scramble about feeding on meat, they will defecate over each other and quickly become chilled. Until their eyes are open you must control all their mealtimes. If they are doing well under your rearing program, they will start to open their eyes at four weeks, and you will then be able to give them two meals a day of whole, rather than scraped, minced beef (around a teaspoonful each). Once you reach this stage, you will be able to cut the milk feedings down to four-hourly intervals, and by the end of the fourth week you should be able to leave them to sleep the night away—bliss! Also, by this time their natural instinct for cleanliness will have taken over and their bowel muscles will be working; they will use the farthest corner of their box to defecate and so remain clean for most of the time. This is a welcome advance.

Once the kits open their eyes you can discontinue the pipette or dropper for their milk feeding and allow them to drink from a bowl. By five weeks they will be capable of feeding entirely on their own, and at six weeks they should be independent and indistinguishable from their naturally-reared contemporaries. When they reach this stage they can, of course, be housed in a normal cage. Do remember that for the first three weeks of their lives the kits will need gentle heat and also that once they open their eyes they will need space to run about and play. You can house them in a large, deep, cardboard box—line it with thick wads of newspaper and cover the bottom with sawdust. Still give them a separate box to sleep in, of course.

This all represents a tremendous amount of work and effort. You need a family prepared to help and support you, for you need some sleep and most of us have to earn a living. My family organized a shift system for the night feedings which worked very well. We ended up rearing eight out of ten; one died and one I put down at two weeks as it was not very strong, but the rest were lovely ferrets. You may wonder if it is worth all the effort. I certainly think it is. The successful rearing of those eight tiny ferrets from four days old to maturity is one of the most rewarding things I have ever done. Over the years the litter has given my family and the friends who own one of them so much pleasure and reward. All other things aside, they grew up to be the most fantastic workers, absolutely steady at all times; they never lie up, and they come when they are called. Imagine having a ferret which stays down a rabbit burrow rather longer than she should, and being able to stick your head down a hole, shout her name and up she comes! I still have three of them, and I value them above rubies.

One final comment on the litter. A friend of mine who has one of the jills was walking through some very high bracken with his jill in her box on his back, when he discovered that the box had opened and the jill had gone. He crouched down to peer about, and, to his surprise, he saw the jill some 30 yards away, working her way toward him by following his line through the thick undergrowth. When she caught up with him she crawled up his leg and back into her box.

CHAPTER **The Hunt is**
FIVE On—Working

Working with ferrets always involves entering your ferret to a hole in the ground and catching whatever comes out. Ferrets are part of a team, and it is after their role has been played that most of the variations take place. You may use nets, guns, dogs or hawks, but by the time any of these comes into play the ferret's job will have been done—for the moment at least. It is up to you as the owner trainer to see that the ferret has the chance to use its natural talents to the full.

Over the years I have made just about all possible mistakes when ferreting, with perhaps one notable exception—I have never lost a ferret. I have come very close to doing so more than once, but have always gone home with a full team, supplemented on occasion by a few extras picked up along the way. Maybe I have been lucky, for I have hunted some big places and done some stupid things; in the main, though, I have always tried to do the job right. If you follow the simple, commonsense rules, you will not go far wrong. Above all, you should know your ferrets well and understand them. Give them plenty of time underground and do not give up on them when they do not surface after ten minutes. It can be an hour or more before anything happens, even if the burrow (often called a bury in Great Britain) looks small, particularly in open downland where the tunnels go many yards down and back into a hillside.

A polecat/ferret hob anxious to enter a netted rabbit hole. The ferret's primary job in hunting is to "bolt"; that is, to enter the hole and chase the rabbits out of their burrows and into carefully prepared nets.

THE QUARRY

Before we get on to the methods used, it may help to say something about the quarry. Most people are well aware that ferrets are used to hunt rabbits and rats. Few, however, realize how many other creatures can be persuaded to move into the open when faced with a working ferret.* For most ferreters the principal quarry is still the rabbit, as was proved by the drop in numbers of ferrets in the 1950's when rabbits were virtually wiped out by myxomatosis. Those of us who are followers of the old ways and traditions in the hunter gatherer mold wish to eat at least some of our catch and therefore set out to catch rabbits. Some two years ago I conducted a survey among several hundred ferreters spread across the whole of the country and found that 85 % hunted rabbits to the exclusion of all else. Of the remaining 15%, all hunted rabbits when the chance came up, but most hunted rats. Less than 2% hunted foxes. The results surprised me, as I had felt that the hunting of rats had perhaps kept the ferret going during the years of myxomatosis and would have been much more popular, but on reflection, if this had been the case the small ferret type would have been predominant. Consequently, I have been left with an unanswered question or two.

Although I have had foxes in my nets on several occasions, I would never intentionally hunt them with ferrets. Few ferreters would, as even the smallest vixen is well able to kill the largest ferret. Whenever I have bolted a fox I have been alone and totally silent; I can only assume that

*Since most states in the U.S.A. ban hunting of any type with ferrets (and hawks), be sure to check your state's hunting regulations before attempting to use a ferret in hunting. Also, the common American rabbits do not burrow but instead build nests on the surface.

it has been sound asleep when the ferret has come up to it. If I really want a fox, I use a terrier and the right-sized net—foxes can make a mess of a rabbit net, believe me.

I have only heard of one other animal, the gray squirrel, being deliberately bolted with ferrets, and I only know of one man who does it regularly. Alan Bryant keeps a ferret especially for the job. As part of his work in pest control, Alan is often called upon to clear squirrels out of roof spaces in suburban houses and garages. Squirrels are bad news in a roof as they can do a tremendous amount of damage. He tells me that they are terrified of his old hob and come out as if the devil were after them! That particular ferret has really taken to squirrel hunting and, if he gets up to them, will kill them very quickly, which is quite an achievement, as a squirrel has a tremendous bite that is far worse than any rat's—and I have been bitten by both.

There are several other creatures which may turn up in your nets and cause some excitement, but they are the exception rather than the rule. When I have been ferreting rats I have only bolted rats, except once when my jills found a hedgehog, but then they did not bolt him—only his fleas! It is when ferreting for rabbits that you come across the unexpected. I have bolted stoats, weasels, cats, little owls and, to date, two pheasants. I have also heard of ferrets bolting a hare and a snake. The hare was bolted by a large hob after giving a small jill such a hiding that she subsequently died. The snake, an adder, was moved out by a jill—they both died. Watch out for the badger. If there is any sign of a hole being occupied by badger do not enter your ferret, for it will be very lucky to come out alive. I have often heard of ferrets being killed by badgers and once I had a terrified jill chased out by an irate badger who came roaring up the tunnel after her.

RABBITING WITH FERRETS AND NETS

Putting aside the oddities, let's return to the essentials of hunting and catching our major quarry, the rabbit. The

Before you go ferreting, allow your jills to practice passing through the nets without pulling them down. Jills are usually set loose down the burrow because they are small and capable of easily passing through the nets. Since the larger hobs would get caught in the nets, they are used as line ferrets. The hobs are put on a leash (or line) and used to retrieve any jills that kill their prey and "lay up" below ground.

ferret is there to bring the rabbits out into the open, not normally to kill them for you. Killing rabbits is an easy task; finding them after your ferret has killed them is not so easy. Whatever method you use to catch the rabbit, the ferret's task in the proceedings remains the same—bolting. After this you take over. You need some means of stopping or slowing down the rabbit's progress as it leaves its hole. Few people are blessed with the lightning-fast reflexes required to grab a bolting rabbit as it rockets by, even assuming that they chance to be in front of the right hole at the right time. Most rabbits are caught in "purse nets," so-called because they close around their victim like a string purse.

If you intend to use purse nets, you need to have enough to cover every hole that you intend to work. No matter how many you have, you always seem to need more. Net-making is a permanent task in my house in spite of my stock of over 300. In addition to purse nets you can use "long nets." These come in many lengths, from the true long net around 100 yards long to shorter versions four or more yards long which are used as gate nets or long-stops on awkward corners and in ditch endings. Many ferreters use a long net set up all around a burrow to catch rabbits bolted from otherwise unrestricted holes, and sporting prints showing warreners at work sometimes show long nets used in addition to purse nets in much the same way. The gate or ditch net can be any length, and when you regularly ferret the same piece of ground you soon become aware of the need, and best length, for such a net.

ADDING DOGS

You may elect to shoot over your ferrets or to use dogs such as whippets, greyhounds and terriers. As a boy, I could have done with a ferret or two to add to the day's sport. Ferretless, I would take my father's gun-trained cocker spaniels rabbiting. My father was not at all impressed with that, as a gun dog commits a cardinal sin if it chases rabbits. My game, however, was a little different from ferreting. I used to sit in the hedgerow, and the dogs, four or five at a time, would keep the rabbits out in the field for me to shoot with a longbow. I must have been quite a shot in those days, as I rarely came home without a rabbit or two.

Rabbiting with dogs can be great fun when you have a steady stream of bunnies bolted out to give the dogs a good course. A great many escape to live another day, but with an intelligent dog the bag can be quite considerable. If you are using small dogs such as whippets, they can be allowed to run free as they can whip round a bush and pick up a rabbit in the twinkling of an eye once they have learned the game. Larger dogs, which cannot turn so fast in confined areas and therefore need a good run, should really be held on a slip leash and only released when the rabbit is well clear of the bushes or hedgerow. A dog who is regularly foiled by the rabbit diving back into cover soon becomes either noisy or bored. It also expends valuable energy running around the bushes trying to find out where its quarry has gone. Hunting by sight, it becomes confused and frustrated. I have seen good dogs ruined by not being given a fair chance, ruined to the extent that they will refuse to run after a rabbit and merely stand watching it go by. Terriers on their own are usually not quick enough to catch rabbits in the open, but two or three at a time running a hedgerow or bramble patch in conjunction with a good ferret underground can produce an exciting day's sport. My own terriers love that kind of day, for it is all action for them and they are busy, busy, busy all day and never seem to tire. As a dog-owner, some of my best sport has been on days such as this. Ferreting with nets can be boring for dogs, who are not allowed to touch the nets or the rabbits.

There is one other method worthy of note—the most exotic, taking you into another area of field sports—and

While the ferrets are underground doing their work of chasing the rabbits from their burrows, you can let your dogs run free to chase the rabbits as they surface. (Dogs can be used either as a "backup system" in the event the rabbits escape from the nets, or in place of the nets.) It is suggested that if you plan to go ferreting with both ferrets and dogs you allow each to get acquainted with the other at an early age.

that is the flying of trained hawks at bolted rabbits. One problem with this sport, apart from the difficulty of obtaining a hawk, is that it can be risky for the ferret, which can so easily end up as hawk-food. Falconry is a difficult sport to get into unless you know someone who is already involved. The right birds are hard to find and expensive. Birds of prey are extremely time-consuming, and it is perhaps a good thing that they are so difficult to obtain, for that goes some way toward ensuring that only those who are really keen to do it properly get the chance to keep and fly them.

CONTROLLING THE FERRETS

It is important to have some control over your ferrets before you start to work them, and this will only come with handling and training. Ferrets actually need little training in the accepted sense of the word; they should take to their work like a bird to the air, for it comes naturally to them. In the early stages of their development they can be spoiled if you go about things in the wrong way, but you would have to be incredibly inept to ruin a ferret's working instinct completely.

I have already mentioned how I give my young ferrets the chance to get used to my feet and the feel of the grass and soil. This is important; unless they have been given the chance to explore, they can be at a loss when you first put them in front of a hole. Before you go out ferreting, try to spend some time getting your ferrets used to the strange things around them; this includes you, the nets they will be expected to pass through without pulling them down and any dogs you may have with you. I use a small pen in my garden, complete with a false burrow. This teaches the ferrets to enter a hole, and with a net sometimes stretched across the holes they learn that they can pass through a net rather than pull it down. In the absence of such a set-up, you can take your youngsters to an unoccupied burrow and let them learn the game by following a more experienced ferret.

In addition, I introduce them to my dogs from a very early age—six or seven weeks. I do not expect my dogs to like my ferrets, or vice versa, but I do expect them to be reasonably relaxed in each other's company. As a matter of interest, my whippet is quite relaxed in the company of the white ferrets but doesn't usually stay too close to the polecats or polecat ferrets. My terriers, however, who much prefer foxing to rabbiting, treat all ferrets with bored disdain and virtually ignore them. Nevertheless, one had been known to be jealous and nip any ferret which she thinks gets too much attention. Dogs which react violently to ferrets are no use when ferreting, and you should beware of claims about docile dogs when working with strangers. You should never allow strange dogs near your ferrets until you are sure of their reaction. Many people have had their ferrets killed by excited dogs, and it is not the way to make friends, especially if your dog is the culprit.

Most important of all is familiarizing your ferrets with being picked up in a working situation. You need to be able to collect your ferrets in a quiet and definite way; if you have not accustomed them to being handled, you can be in for a trying time. An animal which is nervous or unused to its situation will either disappear back down the hole every time you go near or back away into the entrance as you extend your hand to pick it up. In most cases this sulking at the entrance and refusal to emerge can be put down to rough and inconsiderate handling. If you sweep your ferret off its feet and up into the air every time it emerges, it will soon try to avoid you. Ferrets should be taught at an early age to come to you without fear. Young ferrets frequently get all fluffed-up and excited the first time they are worked. You must forgive this reaction on the first few occasions, but once they are fully entered they should behave properly. Do not keep any which continue to get over-excited in spite of careful handling. If you are patient with your ferrets when you first start to work them, the resulting steady and reliable workers will repay you many times over.

If you are just starting with ferrets, you will not have a litter to train; it is more likely that you will be the proud owner of one ferret. Hopefully that ferret will be a youngster bought at about eight weeks of age from a reputable breeder. If this is the case, the advice on handling and training still applies, as you will have to steady your animal before you start. You may, however, have bought an adult animal. In general I would not recommend this, for although you may be lucky enough to obtain a perfect gem of a working ferret, you could find you have bought someone else's failure. Ideally, you should buy your stock between July and October, when most of the current crop of young ferrets is available, and, if possible, you should start with three animals, two jills and one hob, or alernatively two medium-sized hobs. There are only limited situations where one solitary ferret can be used effectively. Normally jills are used as free-running, loose bolters, and the hobs are used to flush out any jill which kill and lay up below ground. Used in this way, hobs are normally worked with a collar and line so that you can keep in touch with them and recover any dead rabbits they may locate when they chase the jills out. If you decide on keeping two hobs only, you can work them loose or on a line. Either way, in your first season you would be well advised to take things slowly and try not to over-reach yourself or your ferrets; keep to small manageable places where you can see what is going on. Leave those vast and fascinating 400-hole sets until you are equipped with the know-how—and the nets.

NETS, BOXES AND OTHER EQUIPMENT

In addition to your ferrets, you will require some equipment. As in any sport, the more involved you become the more equipment you seem to gather around yourself, and you can soon end up bowed under the weight of it all. When ferreting you have to move about any given area quite a bit, and vast piles of gear become an encumbrance. A day's pleasant ferreting can become reminiscent of army maneuvers over grinding assault courses. Nevertheless, there are certain items that you should always have about you.

First on the list is something to put your ferret into. This may seem obvious, but I have seen many would-be ferreters trying to keep a ferret in their shirt or their

One piece of equipment you should not be without is a lightweight but strong box in which to keep your ferrets when they are not working. Boxes are more secure and stay cleaner and drier than sacks or bags.

pocket. While this shows that they may have good tame ferrets, it is not very practical for a full day's ferreting. I prefer a lightweight but strong and comfortable box to bags or sacks of any description. Once they are used to their box, the ferrets will invariably sleep until wanted, and if they do make a noise by scratching at the sides they can be put down out of range. Boxes are far more secure, both from your point of view and the ferrets'; they will not be crushed if stepped or sat on in the general excitement, nor will they have any weak spots through which the ferrets can escape to do some hunting on their own. They are cleaner, drier, offer better protection against bad weather and are less disturbing when you come to move on—the ferret in a sack changes position every time you take a step.

Nets you will need in profusion, and you can either buy or make them. Net-making is a profitable way to spend an evening if you wish to enlarge your stock. I make all of my nets myself, using hemp twine. If you elect to buy them, make sure that you buy only the best quality; they will repay you in the long run. Nets are the largest part of your outlay and will last for years if you look after them. Hemp nets are far superior to nylon nets, provided you look after them and hang them up to dry after use; if you do not you will soon have a stock of rotten nets, but their advantages make this extra care well worthwhile. Hemp nets do not tangle; if caught on bushes they can be pulled off without fear of damage; and they stay where they are put in a wind. Nylon nets, although rot-proof, are susceptible to damage, tend to lift off in a wind and, worst of all, will tangle hopelessly at the slightest excuse, which can be maddening when you are in a hurry to get a net down again after a rabbit has bolted. Hemp nets need only a shake to straighten them out and, although more expensive, are well worth the extra cost. Of course, for only a few dollars you can buy a net-making kit and make yourself about 15 good hemp nets which would cost twice as much in nylon and three times as much ready-made in hemp. You do not have to take into account the cost of your time—after all, it is a hobby! For years I tried to sort out how to make nets and had decided that net-making was not for me, when Frank Goodway showed me the way in about ten minutes. It is easier to demonstrate than to write about, but I will describe the moves later.

Always have a spade handy. The time that you forget to take one is the first time you will need it. The old rabbiter's spade was usually known as a graft. Nowadays they are hard to find and expensive, but a good lightweight, narrow garden spade will serve just as well. Sharpened on the edges as well as the end, a spade can cut through roots and undergrowth. With the spade it is helpful to have a steel prodder to assist in locating the run when digging for a laid-up ferret. It helps to have a lump about four inches from the end so that you can feel when you push through the roof of the tunnel. The ideal instrument—with the addition of the lump—is one of the old boiler-house pokers with ring or T-handles. However, a round steel rod about four feet long and three-fourths of an inch in diameter should be fine; if you heat up the end and strike it blacksmith-style to produce a blip near the end, you will also be able to harden it to give it extra strength.

Billhooks and similar implements have no place in my bag on a day's ferreting. That type of ground-clearing should normally be done several days in advance, but if you have to move to uncleared ground through force of circumstance, then a light hand sickle is an advantage. For general clearing around the holes, I always carry a pair of strong pruning shears. If I am working bramble or bracken patches, I do not normally clear them in advance; I simply cut my way in quietly with the shears and go right ahead. Very often a major disturbance will cause rabbits to move out, and large advance-clearance sessions can mean a wasted day. Rabbits do not go much farther down than one foot when setting up home in a bramble patch (not hedgerows where brambles have encroached). As a result, they come out pretty quickly when the ferret goes in and do not need to be left to settle down too long.

Part of every ferreter's kit, whether he has the animal for it or not, seems to be the collar and line. Too many lines are purchased for my liking. I can almost guarantee that every beginner who comes to me for a ferret already has his collar and line. These would-be ferreters are, not unnaturally, consumed with the fear of losing their animal down the first hole it comes across. Apart from its use when taking a pet ferret for a walk, a line should be used only on an animal trained and worked up for the job.

These days a line is often replaced by an electronic locator. This comparatively expensive piece of equipment can be very effective in skilled hands. It consists of a collar fitted to the ferret, with a small battery-powered transmitter and a pocket-sized receiver which, when waved over the ground where the ferret is laid up, will pinpoint its position. Once you have used the instrument a few times, you will also be able to estimate how far down the ferret is. Apart from being something of a traditionalist and feeling that this device is a departure from the sport and art of ferreting, I am also too cheap to buy one. I can see its value in relation to pest control as a paid exercise, but I don't think it is a vital item for the man who uses ferrets for sport. If you are working the same piece of ground year after year, you are likely to make your sport harder, since every hole you dig results in more dead-ends and lay-ups. With a locator, the temptation to dig as soon as the ferret stops for any length of time is very strong. Often it is better to wait, for things do not always break just when *you* think they should. On the rare occasions that I have used a locator the ferrets have invariably proved to be deeper in than indicated by the signal strength, and I for one would rather wait for my ferret than dig a hole 15 or more feet deep.

One item of equipment which is purchased by almost every beginner, but most definitely has no place in my bag, is a muzzle or cope. Leather and metal muzzles or string copes are no use to any decent working ferret, and if you lose a ferret restricted in this way, you will almost certainly condemn it to a slow death. Admittedly, a string cope can be removed by the ferret if it tries hard enough, but there is always the possibility that a muzzled ferret may come across something more formidable than a rabbit. These considerations apart, a loose ferret will often persuade a reluctant rabbit to bolt by giving it a quick nip in the rear. In addition, a muzzled ferret may spend ages scratching hopefully at a rabbit tucked into a dead-end, whereas a free ferret may kill quickly and then move on, leaving the kill to be located by the line ferret later, particularly if your loose ferrets are well-fed beforehand.

You may find it useful to carry one or two small bells. I no longer use bells on loose ferrets underground. I used to when I first took up ferreting, fitting them to collars made from shirring elastic. In the event of a ferret being caught up underground by its collar, it could quickly free itself. I went through a lot of bells (and elastic) in my first season, but I quickly came to the conclusion that they were a waste of time. I needed to hear the bell not when the ferret was below ground, but when it surfaced in thick cover. The theory was that when the ferret surfaced it would shake itself, ringing the bell and causing me to leap into action to retrieve it from the depths of a bramble patch or whatever. The practice, however, was somewhat different. When the ferret did surface, complete with bell, it rarely shook itself and the bell was invariably clogged with damp soil and thus incapable of emitting more than a dull clonk. Also, the bell would get caught in the meshes of the nets, entangling the ferret hopelessly, which did not do a lot for its temper. I now feel that bells are for hawks, not ferrets, with one exception. In the summer I sometimes use a large hob in conjunction with a terrier to flush rabbits out of thick cover for my whippet bitch. A bell is very useful in large clumps of thick gorse or bramble, as it gives some idea of his location. It is not foolproof, however, as the bell can be left behind and your ferret can drift off, leaving you crawling about trying to see into bushes, wondering if there was a hole in there after all.

And always—but always—carry a knife.

WHEN TO GO FERRETING

Having trained yourself to understand the ways of your ferrets and having gathered together at least the bare minimum of equipment, you are ready to go ferreting. When should you start? In Great Britain the season for rabbiting is never closed, but, for ease when working ferrets, the most usual time is between the months of September and March. Ferreters who use their animals for sport call a voluntary halt during the spring and summer months for a number of reasons. Once the young rabbits start to appear, ferreting becomes difficult because the ferrets will spend all their time catching and killing them. This is non-productive; not only does it spoil the sport, but it also causes lay-ups. It is far better to wait until the little ones have grown up to a usable size. I always feel obliged to take young ones if I have killed their parents, but I do not find it either pleasurable or sporting. The trouble is that in recent years the rabbits, in the south at least, seem to have been breeding all year around. For the last four or five years my son and I have spent New Year's Day ferreting together, and on each occasion we have found a doe heavy with young in our nets, even on New Year's Day 1979, when we were out in three feet of snow. Perhaps the main reason for a break in ferreting during spring and summer is that the growth is up, so rabbit burrows are very difficult to work. Long grass, weeds and bramble growth mask many of the exits, particularly the boltholes, which are often missed even when the ground is clear. If the summer has been very dry and the hedgerow growth has been reduced to a minimum by drought, I may start off in the middle of August, particularly if myxomatosis has started to creep in and thin out my possible chances of clean rabbits later. Otherwise, I stick to the more normal time of late September until early March, with the most productive period being November to January.

It used to be said that it was best to set out with ferrets on a dry, cold, frosty day with little wind. While it is possibly true that rabbits bolt better under such conditions, I go ferreting whenever I am able to, rain or shine. If you are lucky enough to have the right conditions, make the most of them—but if not, go anyway. How often have you woken up to one set of weather conditions, only to find that things have changed by midday? Whatever the weather, remember that rabbits bolt much more readily in the morning, so the earlier you start, the better the day's sport. A friend, Len Brookman, takes out beginners in his capacity as branch secretary of the Ferret Society, and they are often a little taken aback when he tells them what time to be ready. He likes to be on his ground, settled and sorted out, a cup of tea inside him and ready to go almost before it is light enough to see the holes; quiet and unharried, he sets to and usually has a few in the bag before most people are up. In this I am with him all the way, starting at first light and setting the last nets never later than 3 p.m.

APPROACHING THE BURROWS

Once you have arrived at your chosen spot, the next and most important thing is your approach to the burrows. Silence is the thing to aim for, and it is much easier to maintain if you are unhurried. People often discuss methods of approach to a burrow, and I have listened for hours to talk about silent approach into the wind minus cigarettes. Such advice is fine and you should follow it if you can, but of course it is not always possible. Most of my ferreting is carried out in thick hedgerows, woodland, thorn scrub and bramble patches, so if I worried too much about wind direction, half the holes would be left unnetted. Generally, unless the wind is very strong, the scent of man and his cigarettes only percolates slowly, as there is little in the way of strong air movement below ground level. If the wind has been strong for several days and the burrows are left exposed, it is likely that the occupants will have already left for less drafty quarters. You must move around and take your chances. Nevertheless, there is no sense in making difficulties for yourself, so keep the smoking down and spare at least half an eye for the wind direction.

I cannot stress too much the importance of remaining quiet. If you are going to do the job properly, you should be silent not only in your approach but also throughout the whole operation. Talking should be kept to a bare minimum; established partners use hand signals instead. Everyone has his own system of signals, and this can be confusing unless explained to a newcomer beforehand. Out ferreting with two friends who have been partners for years, I discovered halfway through the morning that a small sound made through clenched teeth indicated that movement had been heard below ground. Unfortunately, that same sound is used by me to wind up my dogs when something is afoot above ground. The result was two dogs rushing around looking for the quarry which was still underground. Confusion reigned temporarily. My own signal for such underground bumping is to paddle my hands up and down in front of me—the dogs also know what it means and tense up, waiting for the break.

Anyone who comes out ferreting with me is unlikely to be invited again if he or she insists on yapping away about all and sundry or clumps around like a regiment of foot-guards. My partner on several occasions, Phil Guy, six feet-three inches of grenadier, can give many a smaller man lessons in stealth; he is also agile. More than once I have found myself sitting on the other side of a hedge trying not to laugh out loud as Phil leaped about dealing with rabbits when they hit the nets all at once—the only sound being quiet muttering under his breath. Mind you, we are not always so quiet, particularly when we have just lost what seems to be the only rabbit home out of an undiscovered bolthole! One man I went out with last season was quiet in the ordinary sense but had on a pair of wellingtons which did not fit properly around his legs. Every time he moved, if only to transfer his weight from one foot to another, the boots made a noise like rabbits moving underground. By the end of the morning the poor chap had had us on the hop so many times that he was embarrassed, and we were not ready for the rabbits when they did actually bolt!

WORKING ALONE OR IN COMPANY

As a beginner you would be well advised to have a partner, and even when you are experienced you will generally find the day more enjoyable if accompanied. It is important to find someone you can get on with and whose approach to the business is similar to your own. Many people's whole attitude to the sport is governed by the bag at the end of the day and nothing else. If they have not caught every single rabbit that has bolted or if they have not taken a large number, they have not enjoyed themselves. Such people are not for me. As long as I have one or two rabbits to take home at the end of the day, that's all that matters, and if one or two slip the nets and then manage to slip past the dog as well, they deserve their freedom.

My longest-serving partner is my eldest daughter, Elizabeth, who has been ferreting with me from an early age.

Some women enjoy ferreting. This one, for example, constructs her own nets and skins her own catch!

But all my family are involved at some time during the season. You do not need a large group; the ideal number of people varies with the circumstances, but the maximum for efficient ferreting under most conditions is three. Two are usually enough. You can go ferreting on your own—I have done so many times—but there are few occasions when by yourself you can operate the nets, work the ferrets, take the rabbits from the nets and generally be on top of all that is happening. You are usually restricted to small burrows approachable from one side only or to two- and three-opening burrows around tree stumps, for example. I do enjoy the occasional small expedition when I can carry a dozen nets in my pockets and one tried and trusted jill in a single box. Traveling light like this I can cover a lot of ground, particularly in woodland with a lot of small burrows. At such times rabbiting often takes second place to the joy of walking alone, watching and listening to all that goes on in the quiet of a vast open wood.

LOSING A FERRET

It is when ferreting alone that I seem to do the stupid things we all seem to have to do before we learn anything. On one particular occasion I did something which could easily have cost me a very good ferret. I had taken a large young hob ferret out one day, while on business, in order to show him to some business friends who had never had a close look at a live ferret. To add a little to their knowledge, I had taken along a few purse nets, on the basis that a picture saves a thousand words. Whenever I traveled I took a dog with me, and at lunch times it was my standard practice to take her out of the car for a quick spin over the nearest common or open space. On the day in question we happened to be near a piece of well-wooded common land. Not five minutes from the car, we found a small rabbit burrow with four or five holes—just the number of nets I had with me. Why not give the ferret an airing and maybe take home a rabbit or two, I thought. So I returned to the car, picked up my hob in his big heavy box and wandered back to the little burrow. It was close, but not especially close, to a large blackthorn thicket. I put the ferret into the burrow and stood back. Within seconds there were two rabbits in the nets. A great start, I thought, but after about ten minutes, when my ferret had not shown, I began to wonder. There could be no doubt—he was off into the blackthorn thicket behind me. I started to make a circuit of the thorn, which seemed totally impenetrable, only to discover to my horror that it was something like an acre in extent. I was not dressed to go pushing my way into that lot, as I was wearing a business suit and blackthorn is the worst there is!

I wandered around vaguely peering under the bushes, hoping for a sight of my hob, who would come to his name if in the right mood. I rightly assumed that he would not do so on this occasion, as there were rabbits charging around in all directions and he was having the time of his life. After some time had elapsed, I went back and sat down on his box to work out what to do. Maybe he would eventually come out near where he started, for ferrets often follow their own line back when things have quietened down. I could see part of the way into the bushes, so for want of something better to do I stayed where I was. After sitting for about an hour, with occasional trips around the thicket, I was surprised to see a good-sized fox come galloping straight for me. The ferret had bolted the fox, as a good finish to the show, and came trotting back to where he had left me, looking very pleased with himself. It all sounds clever now, but it was sheer chance that he found me again, for he came back on the surface, not underground. At least I had the sense to sit quietly and wait, my only saving grace in a situation that should never have taken place. If you do ferret alone take care not to overreach yourself; it is all too easy. I am convinced that most of the ferrets I find have been lost by people ferreting alone, especially people who do not have the patience to sit and wait for more than a few minutes for their ferret to come up. When their ferret shows up with an "'ere I am, guvnor" look on its face, they are long gone.

What can you do if you do lose a ferret? There are several courses open to you. If the burrow is very large the ferret could be anywhere, and there is not a lot of point in digging for it. After you have tried to bring it out with other ferrets or with a paunched rabbit, you can try noise or smoke (assuming that you have finished ferreting). Banging the ground with your spade may wake your sleeping ferret below ground, bringing it to the surface to find out what is going on. Smoke, in the form of drain-testing smoke cartridges, is often used to flush reluctant ferrets—I am not keen on this method, but it does work. If, however, you have to go away and leave the animal, assuming you know in which burrow it is you can block off all the entrances and seal it in until you can return the next morning, when the ferret will come up for food. A tunnel trap, suitably baited, can be left in one of the entrances, or the animal's traveling box left in the entrance half-closed will act as an attraction. If you have no spade, smoke, traps or spare boxes, a handful of dry straw or grass stuffed into a closed-up burrow entrance may encourage the ferret to use it as a bed when all the exits are closed; ferrets will rarely dig themselves out if you close them in tight.

SETTING THE NETS

We now come to perhaps the most important part of ferreting: the setting of the nets. Most ferreting is carried out with nets and, if you are to succeed, you must set them properly. The real experts take ages to set them, so you should not hurry over the task. Nets seem to have a life force all their own and will do their best to help the quarry escape if you do not pay sufficient attention. Take the net from your bag and straighten it out, with the top ring and the peg held in your hand. Place the bottom end of the net into the entrance of the hole and push the bottom ring lightly into the soil—just hard enough to check it slightly. Still holding the top ring, push the peg into the soil above the hole and then spread the net over the hole, making sure that it neither hangs in folds nor stretches tight. It should cover the edges but be free to run up without being caught on any obstruction. This is not always easy, partic-ularly when operating in tree roots, where nets will snag at every opportunity. If the net is set correctly, and if the rabbit hits it straight on, it should close smoothly around its victim every time. Anyone can set a net over a neat, obstruction-free hole and catch a rabbit, but it needs a bit more skill and consideration when the holes are in thick cover or when, as is often the case, they are enlarged caves with several entrances running away in all directions. Rabbit holes rarely run straight back into the ground; therefore, the bolting rabbit very frequently hits the net at quite an acute angle. It is then that you will find out if you have arranged the net properly. In some places, like steep slopes or cut-back sandbank entrances, it is difficult to get the spread-out net to stay in place. The edges of the net can be held open by pushing small pieces of twig, sometimes known as prickers, into the soil on either side of the hole and lightly hanging the net on them.

Three stages in setting a purse net. Hemp twine is far superior to nylon as a net material. Hemp nets are expensive, but they do not tangle as easily as nylon nets and are well worth the money.

Not all rabbit holes are as neat and uncluttered as those shown on the opposite page. It takes more skill and time to set nets over holes that are located in thick brush, as shown here.

111

On the subject of nets, you will find that there is much controversy about the choice of color. Should you use green nets, brown nets or even blue nets to match the sky against which the rabbit sees them? Frank Goodway has nets of every hue imaginable in his net bag—green, blue, orange, all sorts. I once questioned him on his choice of color, and his eminently sensible answer was that he had yet to find a rabbit that complained about it. In fact, a rabbit is unlikely to be able to see the net until it is too late; it does not have forward-facing eyes. A cone-shaped blind spot in its forward vision prevents it from seeing anything directly in front of it closer than 12 feet. This gives it little chance of seeing the net before it is too late—in theory, at least. In practice, however, many holes emerge into a cave-like entrance or at an acute angle which gives the rabbit a chance to see the net from the side. Put all these theories from your mind, however, for, when viewed from inside the hole, a net is seen only in silhouette against the sky or the background of woodland, and its color matters little. A rabbit approaching a net for the first time is unlikely to associate it with a trap and will ignore its silhouette. If it is caught in a net and escapes, it is reluctant to pass through one a second time if it comes up to it slowly. I have seen rabbits sitting just inside a hole move forward and slowly push their way into a net when they have not had previous experience, and I have also seen rabbits run into a clearly visible net from the outside when pressed, after previously escaping from a badly set net. On a recent occasion, I removed a half-grown rabbit from a net and released it, only to see it run into a net again three times before I finally persuaded it to clear off to another burrow out of harm's way. The only thing I bother with when it comes to color is the draw line, which should be white. White drawlines enable you to see the edges of your nets when you are laying them down, and they also help you to find the nets again when the time comes to pick

A properly set purse net such as this one will prevent the quarry from escaping. "Purse net" is an appropriate name, since it closes around the prey like a string purse.

them up. Fine nylon nets are extremely difficult to find without a distinctive drawline, and nets are too expensive to leave behind.

I was once told that I should use white nets when ferreting in the snow: maybe the object of that exercise was to add to the fun at the end of the day—a sort of sporting hunt the thimble! My nets are mainly the natural greeny-brown of the hemp string from which I make them; in addition I have, over the years, collected a fair selection of colors, a great many of which have been picked up after being left by someone else. It is not always easy to remember just how many you have laid on any particular burrows, especially when the numbers go into treble figures. My own method is not infallible but a great help. To start with, I know how many nets I take out, how many are in each bag and where the extra-large ones for big holes are. The nets are prepared the night before to make sure that they are all clean and sound, free from bits of rubbish and tightly fixed to their pegs. After checking, each is folded twice, end-to-end, and laid against the peg. I then attach the net to the side of the peg by putting a small rubber band over the whole thing, which holds the net tidy until required. As I set each net, I take the rubber band off and slip it over one of my fingers. When I come to pick up the nets, I know how many were laid by the number of bands on my finger. One left means one net still down somewhere! By spending a few seconds putting rubber bands on the nets and then taking them off, you will ensure that each net is always ready for use, and you should end up with the number of nets you set out with.

Once I have arrived at the burrows, I always set the nets before doing anything else. If you have sufficient, it is well worth netting up several burrows before you start, as this gives the first one or two burrows time to settle down again before you enter the ferrets. In addition, it adds to your chances of catching any rabbit that bolts from a missed exit or slips out of a net, for it will probably be back-netted if it tries to enter a burrow you have set ahead. For this reason, I also leave the nets down over the last worked burrow when moving on. Once a rabbit has back-netted itself, providing your peg holds tight, that rabbit is going nowhere but into your gamebag. If you leave rabbits in nets on the surface for very long, they will be out and away, but to date I have never had a rabbit back out of a net once it has taken it below ground; it will sit there, pushing hard, in an attempt to get through the net and further underground. The only problem is that you might not see it go, and then you can easily miss the net, for all that can be seen is a bit of tight drawline and your peg. If a rabbit slips out of a net and then goes to ground in a fresh burrow nearby, you will have a job to shift it again unless you are quick. Once you give a bolted rabbit a chance to settle with its head in a corner, you will never shift it again that day. If you are quick and the burrow is small, you just might get it out, but it is rarely worth a try.

LET THAT ODD RABBIT GO

On one of our New Year's Day expeditions my son Michael and I were ferreting on the North Downs. There had been a heavy fall of snow overnight and in places the level snow was three feet deep, so we were traveling light, with only the ferrets and a few nets. Indeed, we had to drive the car backward up some of the hills because the roads were still covered in virgin snow and we could make no progress going forward. Getting out of the blast of the north wind, we decided to set out nets on a south-facing slope in a small beech wood; within seconds we had the first rabbit in the bag, and moments later the only other occupant in the small burrow was in a net. As Michael picked it up, he slipped in the snow and fell flat on his face. The rabbit slid through his fingers like an eel and shot away up the bank and into an unnetted burrow about 25 yards away. As we were unlikely to find many that day and we had come a long way, every one counted. There were only four holes in the burrow, so we slapped the nets down quickly and entered a good jill who had never once killed a rabbit. For over two hours that one rabbit rattled around the burrow, and every time it came to nets it turned back in over the jill, who was getting a good kicking all the while. While my son went on to other burrows, I stood there up to my knees in snow on bone-hard ground, freezing to death and cursing myself for being so stupid. In the end I admitted defeat, lifted my nets and called my jill out. Unless you are working a burrow where there are several other rabbits, it is never worth trying to get one particular lone rabbit; it is better to lay nets and back-net the loose ones.

Not every ferreting expedition of mine turns into a chapter of accidents! I could bore you with stories of successful days when everything has gone according to plan and the resulting bag has been memorable, but, in the main, the days that first spring to mind are either those on which everything has gone wrong, or the ones that have turned into something of a comedy act.

PREPARING THE GROUND

A few days before setting out loaded with equipment, ferrets and high hopes, you should try to spend some time going over the ground you intend to work, clearing excess growth from around the entrances of the burrows and generally spying out the lay of the land. This will reduce the chances of things going wrong and is particularly important when you are going to work a piece of ground for the first time. The old army saying that "time spent on reconnaissance is never wasted" is a great truth. I rarely have time to check over old ground these days, but I always make a point of walking over any new territory. On one occasion I was asked to go and clear a piece of ground and on arrival walked around, only to find that the huge rabbit burrow I had been told about was, in fact, a large and fully occupied badger set. I told the landowner just what his tenants were, and he then took me to yet another burrow which turned to be the largest fox-earth I have ever seen. There were at least 40 openings, and the entrances of six or eight of them were covered with duck wings. Not every rabbit is a rabbit it seems, any more than the "thousands of rabbits" you are told about can be relied on to produce vast bags.

If you come across a set of holes which you suspect are inhabited by badgers, it would be sensible to leave them alone. If you do try to enter your ferrets to an occupied set, most often they will not go in, or if they do they will not go far before coming out highly ruffled. If your ferret is unlucky enough to come up to a badger, it is unlikely to come back again. You can usually tell when a set is occupied, for if you cast around near the entrances you will find the dung pits, unlike a fox-earth which you have to check on by taking a good sniff. Most badger sets are ancient and cover large areas. Some time ago, when ferreting a farm near Selborne, the home of the naturalist-parson Gilbert White, I found an occupied set which had been dug into a chalk bank separating two fields, one field being some 30 feet above the other. The set extended along the whole length of the bank, which was over 200 yards long, with dung pits every few yards, and although there was also plenty of evidence of rabbits, I did not try to enter my ferrets and left that area empty-handed.

Whenever I walk the ground beforehand I take my dogs, as they can show me so much that I would otherwise miss. They can find isolated burrows in large areas of thick scrub, putting out sitting rabbits, which often gives me an idea which way loose rabbits are likely to run and they point out covered boltholes. Disguised boltholes can be extremely difficult to find, especially when under a lot of dead leaves or dried grass cover. Len Brookman and I once set over 70 nets on one burrow on a golf course, being bombarded all the time by golf balls bouncing off the trees over our heads. The only three rabbits home all left line astern out of the bolthole we had missed.

Very often rabbits will escape from a hole which was not there at the time you laid your nets. Many holes are excavated from the inside; they show up as small exits, sometimes only about two and a half inches across. Frequently at the end of a single tunnel, they appear out in a field, some distance from a burrow in a hedgerow. Occasionally there is no actual exit prepared until a rabbit is hard-pressed, when it may quietly dig its way through, breaking out and nipping off like an escaping prisoner of war tunneling under the wire. It is then that a good dog can come into its own, provided it is paying attention, for a dog will hear the movement and can warn you.

DOGS AS BEATERS AND LONG-STOPS

With correct training a dog can be a great asset. I use mine in two distinct ways: with ferrets and nets they act as beaters and long-stops, while without nets their role is mainly picking up. At present I have two dogs, a terrier and a whippet, who form the perfect team, one for cover and one for open. On a good day they work together like clockwork, the terrier in cover and the whippet circling on the outside waiting for the break. They tend to get bored with ferreting if there is too little for them to do. On such days the terrier is liable to clear off and do a bit of freelance work with the local fox population, and my whippet has been known to creep into one of the ferret boxes and go to sleep. But, if things are going well and rabbits are on the move, they pay attention and rarely miss a trick; few loose rabbits get past them, and those that do are often headed into a back-netting situation.

When working with nets, you must keep dogs out of the way—both of mine know very well that they are not allowed to go near the entrances to rabbit holes before, during or after the setting of nets. Their main job is to act as long-stops, and I will not allow them to go poking their noses into holes before I start working. They are, however, used to "dog in" before the nets are set, moving rabbits that are sitting out on the surface. This can be an important job in my area, as much of the ground is rough thorn scrubland with coarse tussock grass on sloping downland. Over recent years the weather has rarely been bad enough during the season to keep the rabbits below ground, and if I did not dog in I would be hard put to make a reasonable bag.

In the summer, as I mentioned earlier, I use my dogs and ferrets without nets. This type of ferreting can be great fun. Silence is not so vital, as I am working a ferret as a terrier, on the surface only, in very thick cover. I use a big hob for this job. My white hob, weighing over four pounds, is nearly as easy to spot in cover as a small terrier, and this, together with his chatter and the bell on his collar, means that he is easy to follow. If you try this game you must have dogs which are fully broken to ferrets, for they will often come face to face in the middle of a bush. You must keep a look out for any burrows hidden in the growth, or your ferret will go to ground unexpectedly. At that time of year, you could be faced with a long lay-up if he kills and stays in, which being a big strong line ferret he is liable to do. It is well to know your ground, or a pleasant summer stroll could turn into hard work.

KILLING BELOW GROUND

Sooner or later most ferrets will learn to kill their quarry below ground. Some learn early in their first season, others take a couple of years to do so—I have two or three jills who have never killed in over four seasons. It is this act of killing which so often frustrates owners, causing them to consider the use of a muzzle or a line and harness. What is particularly irritating is the ferret which not only kills but lays up, eating its victim and then going off to sleep. There is no certain way of stopping this, but you can reduce the risk. First of all, make sure that your ferrets are well-fed the night before you set out; if you starve them you can expect them to turn the first rabbit they meet into a meal. If you are starting early in the morning, give them a drink of milk when you wake them up and before you put them into their traveling boxes; if you are late starting out, give them a light snack to take the edge off their hunger. Believe me, you will not take the edge off their enthusiasm. When you stop for a break at lunchtime, give the ferrets a drink and a light snack in the form of a piece of rabbit liver, for it is in the afternoon that lay-ups most frequently occur, when the ferrets are getting tired and hungry. Be quiet in your approach and in your method of working, and when you have set your nets, give things time to settle down before you enter the ferrets. Do not put too many down at one time and do not keep poking around in an effort to find out what's going on—keep still and quiet and give the ferrets a chance to take their quarry by surprise which is more likely to make them bolt cleanly and quickly.

Sometimes ferrets can be down in an apparently small burrow for what seems to be a long time. It is not uncommon for a pair of ferrets to be working away for half an hour or more before any rabbits move out; rabbits know their own burrow best and can often run rings around the ferrets without coming out. So do not immediately jump to the conclusion that your ferret is laid up with a kill. If it has been properly fed it should kill and move on. If a ferret has blood around its mouth when it comes up you will know that it has killed. You should also examine the feet of any ferret that has been down for a long time, for if it has had a rabbit that was tucked head-first into a corner the claws will be full of fur, often called fleck. This may not indicate a kill but it may be worth a run through with the line ferret.

USING A LINE FERRET

Most usually the loose workers of your team will be jills, with the occasional small or medium-sized hob. Larger hobs are incapable of passing through the nets without first disturbing them; therefore they are usually kept as line ferrets. A ferret must have several attributes, both physical and mental, before being considered for the job of line ferret. Pure size is not the only qualification required. He must be strong enough to carry the line underground often for considerable distances, pulling it around corners, over roots and up and down the levels of the underground maze. He must be fairly belligerent with his own kind (not with you), for he should be able to drive any laid-up ferret off the kill, sending it back to the surface with a flea in its ear. But mainly he should be brave—brave enough to stay with the kill or, as often happens, a rabbit or rabbits trapped in a dead-end by the loose ferret, awaiting the coming of the spade. Take care when you dig: many good line ferrets have been killed by some over-enthusiastic idiot with a spade.

Having made the decision to use your line ferret, whether because a loose ferret has killed or because one has not shown for a long time, you should attach his line to him by either a collar or a harness. This should not be the first time that he has felt the restriction of line or collar; he should be well used to both. It does no harm to leave a collar on a line ferret all the time, although I would not make a practice of leaving a harness on him, for the sake of his own comfort. The line must be a kink-free cord about 12 yards long. I use a strong white nylon cord which is both light and easy to see in the soil when you break through at any point. It needs to be marked off at one yard intervals so that you will know just how far he has traveled. Do not use knots in the line as they are just one more way of helping the line to get caught up. Dabs of colored dye are probably best; if you can remember the code you could use different colors to tell you how far the line has been pulled in, but it is sufficient to count off the marks as they pass through your hands.

Put the line ferret down in front of the selected entrance. As he goes to ground, pay the line out steadily, preferably off some form of spool, keeping tension on it all the time. You must never let the line go slack or it may become caught in a root or stone underground. If the ferret backtracks you must reel it in, like playing a fish. Do not pull on it to such an extent that the hob has to lean into his collar like a dray horse; just keep it tight.

Which hole do you put him down first? If you have a loose ferret still below ground, then put him down the hole at which it last showed or the hole nearest any action heard or observed. If the loose ferret has come up, then put him down the hole it came up.

Once your line ferret has stopped, having located the kill and, if necessary, having sent up the laid-up ferret, you can start thinking about how you are going to get him out again, along with the rabbit or rabbits you sent him after. It is now that a locator really comes into its own, for it can save you a lot of work. On the rare occasions that I have used a locator, I still used a line on my ferret, for if the locator had failed, which has been known to happen, I would still have had contact via the line. Assuming you are using a locator, you cast about until you find the center of your signal and then proceed to dig down to one side of his position—otherwise you could easily chop your hob in half with the spade. Give him room. Once you have used a locator a few times, you will be able to gauge just how far down your line ferret is from the strength of the signal and dig accordingly. It is wise to check the signal at intervals to make sure he hasn't moved off, especially when he is new to the job.

If you do not have a locator, then you must resort to the time-honored method and cut a length of bramble. Take a long flexible piece, strip it of its thorns with a pocketknife and then use it to trace the direction of the tunnel along which the line is running. When you have established this you can use your steel prodder. By careful prodding and digging you can follow the line until you come to your line ferret on the kill. This can be hard work, depending on the type of ground (obviously, if you are ferreting on rocky ground it is impossible), but it can be rewarding. I am not the only ferreter who has dug down to a line ferret to find that he is holding not one but several rabbits in a dead-end. I have talked to men who in the great days of ferreting, before myxomatosis, found as many as twenty rabbits blocked up in this way. This build-up of rabbits with nowhere to go has been caused, very often, by the loose ferrets driving the rabbits before them along a hedgerow burrow.

If you put your ferrets in only very small burrows you will never need the services of a line ferret, but if you work places with more than half a dozen openings there will come a time when you will need to send one in. It seems to be the middle-sized burrows with 20 or 30 outlets that produce the lay-ups. They are not big enough for the rabbits to move around and around in front of the ferrets and yet not small enough to make them bolt straight off.

THE NUMBER OF FERRETS NEEDED

As I mentioned earlier, the number of ferrets you enter in any particular place is relevant. There are no hard-and-fast rules about this. It is largely a question of experience and intuition. It does not follow that because you are working a huge burrow with several hundred outlets you have to enter six or eight ferrets, any more than that a burrow with under ten holes needs only one ferret. Much depends on the depth of the burrow and the extent of its underground workings, and that is something you can never really know. However, on chalk or hard ground where the rabbits can be heard on the move underground, you will often be amazed at the extent of the tunnels. In firm ground, such as the old chalk downs that I work so often, burrows may be a great age, never filling in even after years of limited occupation. I once put a jill into a burrow which had only two holes about four or five feet apart, and I could hear the rabbits thumping around like distant thunder for over 40 feet back into the hillside in several directions. I became so fascinated by this that I marked out the line of the tunnels that I knew existed and measured them. That one small burrow had at least 250 yards of tunnel. Bear that in mind next time your ferret is down for more than a minute or two.

If small burrows can produce tunnels of that magnitude, imagine how far some of the larger ones extend. When you hunt in large burrows you need several ferrets, and they must be fit. However, fit ferrets or not, there are some places where it is obvious that you do not have the necessary animals or nets. It may not just be the sheer size; it may also be the type of cover which hides the entrances. I hunt one or two pheasant shoots where I must not cut down the undergrowth to get at the rabbits. To do so would destroy the holding cover or the flushing points for the birds, and I would quickly become less than popular. In such circumstances it is wiser to try "stinking out." This method of harassing rabbits is often used by "rough shooters" and gamekeepers in an attempt to keep rabbits on the surface before carrying out a rabbit drive. It is the only way they can ensure that there are enough rabbits above ground after the first few shots to make the drive worthwhile. Two or three days before ferreting you should stuff loose bundles of newspaper soaked in kerosene into the holes in the burrows that you wish to clear, leaving at least one hole in each burrow unplugged so that the occupants can get out. Pay particular attention to the holes on the side of any prevailing wind, for although there is little air movement below it does help the stink of kerosene to percolate further into the burrow. The object in this case is not to keep the rabbits on the surface but to drive them out of the large or inaccessible burrows and into more convenient and easily worked places. This method can often save effort and can be very productive if carried out properly.

THE FERRETING CODE OF BEHAVIOR

Like most ferreters, you will probably be working on other people's ground by invitation, and you do have to follow an accepted code of behavior. Apart from the obvious courtesies like shutting gates and not leaving

When approaching the burrow, stay quiet and still and give your ferrets plenty of time to work underground. Don't poke around in an effort to see what is happening below.

litter—the normal country code—there are one or two other things you must remember if you wish to be invited back. Any holes you dig to retrieve ferrets should be properly filled in before you move on, and any fence posts you have to remove should be properly replaced. Make sure you collect all your nets, particularly where there are cattle; curious young heifers take a delight in eating nets if you give them the chance. If you lose a ferret or have to leave it down, always let the landowner know. Who knows, he may find it for you, and if he keeps hens I am sure you would rather he did not find it in his hen house. If you let him know he is at least forewarned and can shut his hens up tight.

Besides filling in holes that you have dug it is often useful to fill in the entrances of each of the burrows as you go. On your next visit you can check to see which burrows have been opened up by the rabbits and thus save yourself hours of fruitless netting, especially in an area with long hedgerows full of holes where rabbit numbers are low. Do not cut holes in hedges and never leave wire down. One other thing, rather obvious but often forgotten, is to say thank you to the landowner. As my father used to say, politeness costs nothing. It also helps to leave the odd brace of nice, clean, paunched rabbits hanging on his doorknob. Make sure that you choose a door which is in frequent use though; a friend of mine once left a brace on an unused side door of a farmhouse, and by the time the farmer found them they were really humming.

KILLING YOUR RABBITS

One thing which I have not covered yet is how to dispatch your rabbits once you have caught them. The object is to kill them very quickly and cleanly. There are several methods of dispatching rabbits, and perhaps the best known is the method I like least of all—the rabbit punch. A blow is struck at the base of the neck in a downward direction while the rabbit is held up by its back legs. Frequently the first karate-like chop does not strike home in the right place; rabbits do not always oblige you by keeping still. Very often a rabbit is only stunned, as several ferreters have discovered after an apparently dead rabbit has recovered and run off. In addition there is also a certain amount of bruising of the meat around the shoulders. Some practitioners of this method are skilled at killing their rabbits with the minimum of fuss and bruising, but most are not.

By far the best method of killing rabbits quickly and quietly is the method known as chinning up. The rabbit is killed on the ground while it is still in the net. It is held down with one hand on its shoulders, the fingers being spread on either side of the nape of the neck, and the chin is then pushed up sharply backward with the heel of the other hand. If done correctly this dislocates the neck, killing the rabbit in an instant. Once the rabbit is dead you can put it quickly to one side and set a fresh net over that hole in case another one is close behind. You can then take the dead rabbit out of the net in your own good time. An alternative method which involves breaking the neck is to stretch the rabbit out, with one hand holding the back legs and the other holding it behind the head; when the body is pulled out straight the neck is twisted up and sideways with the same end result. The rabbit needs to be removed from the net for this, which can take some time when it is struggling. One other method possible with the rabbit still in the net, and one that is very quick, is to use a priest—not a clergyman but a weighted stick such as fishermen use. In recent years this has also found favor with many shooting men as a method of dispatching game. Struck over the forehead, the rabbit is killed very fast indeed, and it has the advantage of not damaging any part of the meat. Whichever method you use, kill cleanly and humanely.

Having killed your rabbit, you should then "water it":

press your thumb downward toward the vent, with the rabbit held head up, expelling the contents of the bladder. You can then "leg" it and hang it up in a cool place. To leg a rabbit, take a sharp knife and cut a slit between the bone and the tendon on one of the back legs above the hock. Then without damaging the flesh pass the other foot through the slit until the hock joint protrudes through. This joins the back legs together so that you can hang up the rabbit head-down without the need for string. Unless it is very warm I never paunch (gut) any rabbit until the end of the day, when I do them all at once, dropping the unwanted intestines into a pit and filling it in afterward. The only exception I make to this is when I have a possible lay-up, when a freshly killed and paunched rabbit waggled about in the entrance can sometimes produce the desired effect and draw out a ferret.

The methods of ferreting so far described are ones where you can work alone if necessary. True, you need to keep your wits about you when you are alone, but there is no doubt that you quickly become attuned to what is going on around you, and you will find that you soon develop a hair-trigger reaction in which every small movement, such as the blowing of a leaf on the edge of your vision, can make you jerk around. With the variations now to be discussed, however, you should always have someone with you.

SHOOTING OVER THE FERRETS

After ferreting with nets, the shooting of rabbits over ferrets comes out as a clear second favorite. Many shooting men were first introduced to their sport in this way, and certainly if you enjoy shooting it can be great sport. Most keepers who become involved in ferreting as part of their job of rabbit control—during the first three months of the year, between the end of the pheasant-shooting season and the beginning of the rearing season—seem to prefer shooting to netting. If you have the opportunity to involve yourself in that kind of exercise then do so, for it can produce some good results. On keepered ground where game thrives, everything else thrives along with it.

The ideal team is three: two with guns and the third to work the ferrets. The man working the ferrets should not, under any circumstances, carry a gun; his sole responsibility is the effective working of the ferrets and nothing else. Without nets to worry about, he can keep his ferrets on the job, moving with them as they progress through the burrows. High on the list of priorities is gun safety, and generally if you are with professional men you can be pretty sure that you and your ferrets are safe. Safe guns are important everywhere, but with the kind of instant snap-shooting that goes on when rabbits are bolting from ferrets it is very important for a gunner to know what he is doing and for a ferreter to know whether or not one of the gunners is going to get carried away and blow his head off. I do not really like shooting over my ferrets (I prefer the quiet of nets), but when I do go, I make doubly sure that everyone knows what they are doing and where everyone is—particularly me and my ferrets. I will not have anyone shoot along the line of a hedge. Each gun should be placed so as to allow the rabbits to get well clear of the burrow before a shot is taken, and I prefer to see one gun standing close to the hedge on one side and the other to be placed well out to take the rabbits when they are in clear sight of all.

Shooting over ferrets is often a short affair lasting only a morning rather than all day. Because of the time saved by not having to set nets you can cover a lot more ground in less time, unless you get a lay-up or two to slow things down.

What type of shotgun should you use? Many people like a .410, but as most are heavily choked the skill needed is considerable. The majority of shotgunners now use 12-gauge guns, and an open-bored gun coupled with a light load of size six or seven shot are the best gun and cartridge for the job. Because of the type of terrain, the shots frequently have to be taken close up, and a heavy-load cartridge used in conjunction with a choked barrel will produce a carcass not worth picking up. Two friends of mine who are keen on shooting and good shots into the bargain both use guns that are very open-bored—almost true cylinder—for rabbit shooting. So open in fact are the guns that when taking part in a clay shoot some time ago with their beloved hammer guns, they were asked to withdraw as they both kept hitting two clays with one shot. The organizers were understandably upset as it made the whole thing nonsense. They may not be admired on the shooting grounds with their old gas-pipes, but they can produce the goods when there are rabbits about.

FALCONS WITH FERRETS

For me, the most exotic sport involving ferrets is that of flying trained falcons at quarry. Naturally, the quarry is still mostly rabbits, although rats do not come amiss to a falcon. Sadly it is a sport which fewer and fewer people seem to be able to indulge in because of the difficulty of obtaining a license to hold a bird in the first place. Apart from this problem there is also a small matter of money. The cost of purchasing a bird suitable for the task of taking rabbits or similar-sized game is very high. The birds themselves come in two basic types: the long-winged, black-eyed falcons and the short-winged, yellow-eyed hawks. Of the short-winged birds the favorite seems to be the goshawk, although the Harris hawk from the U.S.A. is gaining ground very fast. Of the long-wings, everyone's image of the wild free falcon is the peregrine. Very few people can afford the latter and even fewer can fly it to game because the terrain is rarely suitable. When a peregrine is flying properly it needs lots of space around it, not so much for its own sake but for the sake of the falconer, who needs to be able to see it if it takes off after quarry which it has spotted several miles away.

Long-wings, however, are rarely used for rabbits; falcons mostly catch their quarry in the air. More often the bird used over ferrets is the goshawk, a short-winged bird of the woods which flies in short devastating rushes off the fist to its quarry. To take up such a bird yourself you need to have had experience with other smaller and less explosive characters, starting with a very steady and phlegmatic small falcon, such as the kestrel, and working up via that miniature version of the goshawk, the sparrow hawk. Once you have learned to handle and maintain these two you are then considered ready to go on to greater things and try the goshawk. I am no expert and have never owned a goshawk myself, but I have watched others fly them. Although they are well-named "kitchen hawks" for their ability to keep the kitchen supplied with fresh meat, they can be difficult and ill-tempered birds at times.

Lex Hedley, a well-known and respected falconer in New Zealand, tells me that there is only one native bird in his homeland which is suitable for flying to quarry, the Australasian harrier. Lex flys his birds mostly to rabbits, which are plentiful, and like a great many falconers uses ferrets to bolt the rabbits. Falconers often see ferrets as a means to an end, as second fiddle to the proud hawk on the fist. This is not so with Lex, who gets as much pleasure from his ferrets as he does from his birds.

When using birds of prey with ferrets it is wise to accustom the birds to their presence; otherwise, when the ferret pops up, down will stoop your mighty bird, and you will be in the market for another ferret. Even with care, falconry can be heavy on ferrets. Lex places his animals in wire pens at the back of his harriers' weathering blocks in an attempt to show the birds the ferrets over a long period. This does seem to work, as to date he has not lost a ferret to a bird. Birds of prey are, in the main, very bright; as well as picking up bad habits very quickly, they will also learn good habits if properly taught. Once wedded to their legitimate quarry they will usually stick to it, and it is amazing how fast they learn.

Though I shall probably never have the time to train a real hard-flying bird, I have at present a number of kestrels, including a road-accident victim—a haggard falcon who came to me with a damaged right eye which has since shrunk to nothing. She has whetted my appetite for the world of birds again after a break of 30 years. She has proved to be very intelligent, being completely at ease with me and my dogs after a remarkably short time. It says a lot too for the steadiness of my dogs, who will have a go at most things that move, but will lie out in the garden on either side of the bird as she suns herself on the weathering block. She has become so blasé that she will lie on the grass between them without any worries, wings stretched out like a pigeon. My whippet, who is not above catching a pheasant in the air if my back is turned, makes no attempt to worry her, merely touching noses when they meet. I have heard of the affinity between desert hawks and salukis—but whippets and kestrels? One thing is certain, however: that falcon is safe from any marauding cats, with my dogs lying beside her.

If you have the luck to come by a small hawk in a legal manner and have proper advice on looking after it, then you will be able to use it as a stepping-stone to a new sport. The flying of hawks is a pure sport and a source of great pleasure. Like hunting with hounds, the pleasure comes not from the bag at the end of the day but in watching the bird fly and work free.

RAT HUNTING

So far I have concentrated on hunting the rabbit, but it is now time to get down into the rough, tough world of hunting the rat. With their ability to carry disease and their unpleasant characteristics, rats are greatly disliked by most people. Think carefully before you expose yourself, your ferrets and your dogs to the risks—see the section on leptospirosis in the last chapter of this book.

But after fox hunting and shooting driven pheasants have been stopped, the rat will still be hunted. Imagine the conversation between Lord A and Sir George B: "I say, George! Do you know, I put down 500 brace of well-reared rats last spring and the damned poachers have swiped the lot!" Hardly likely really, for rats left to their own devices would soon take us over.

Of the two species in Great Britain, the black rat is now rare and local, ousted by the larger and more powerful brown rat, which can be found just about everywhere. Most people who hunt rats regularly with ferrets do so for lack of other quarry. It seems from my aforementioned survey that the majority of rat-hunters live in the big cities, where there are very few wild rabbits. The dock-lands of Liverpool, Hull and London are favorites with ferreters who look for rats, as are the rubbish dumps of other major cities such as Birmingham and Manchester. Ratting ferrets need to be small, neat and quick, with the emphasis on quick. Probably jills are best for the simple reason that the average hob is too large to enter the rat hole. The rat is brave, resourceful and very much an even match for a good jill ferret if it should choose to stand and fight. There is every chance of a blood-and-guts battle when ferret and rat meet, so you need to exercise some care when your normally docile jill surfaces fresh from the wars in a rat hole. You should let her know that you are there and offering no threat before you pick her up, otherwise you may find that you have a ferret grafted onto your thumb. Ratting ferrets used regularly become pretty sharp; they need to if they are to survive for long.

Few jills will continue to go to ground after rats willingly for more than one season. It all depends on how often you use them of course, but they tire of the battle after a time; when they begin to show reluctance, that is the time to stop. Ferrets are often injured quite badly in their fights with rats which are cornered or which refuse to bolt because they are defending young. Never force your ferrets to ground. Terrible wounds around the face are common, and the loss of an eye is not unusual. Because of this, I do not often use my jills on rats these days, limiting my forays to less than a dozen times in a year. More often I take my dogs hedgerow-hunting for rats, a sport which they enjoy almost more than anything else.

Ratting with ferrets is exciting, of course, especially in a confined space. Some of the situations you get yourself into with rats can make your hair stand on end—afterwards. At the time you have little or no chance to think because of the speed at which things happen. Rats move like greased lightning, bobbing, ducking and weaving, and it is best to have a good dog or two with you, for you cannot hope to stop them all yourself. The dogs must be taught the difference between rats and ferrets very thoroughly; excited dogs will chop a ferret before they know it themselves if the action is fast and furious, as it ought to be if the rats are there in any number. A rat-hunting stick is handy when the rats start to show. This is a short stick about 18 inches long with a diameter of around one inch. I have a couple of sticks roughly this size which also have a slight "set" in them about halfway down their length. This means I can get down and hit a rat on the ground without banging my knuckles at the same time. People get carried away when killing rats and will often hit your dogs, your ferrets and you in their excitement—so beware!

When I was about 14 years old, I was invited to a rat session at the home of a schoolfriend. His grandfather had a chicken coop in the back garden which had a fair-sized rat colony underneath. The coop was surrounded by a wire fence some six feet high and 12 feet square, and it confined about ten or 12 pullets. The idea was to move it over, disturb the rats and deal with them before they could leave. The old boy impressed on us the need to deal speedily with the rats as they emerged, for, as he pointed out, once in the open they would be off through the two-inch wire-netting like rockets. It took six or eight of us to pick up and move the coop, and we exposed an area of soft ground with several holes and half tunnels. Grandfather started to turn over the soil with a spade, and out came the rats. Everyone started leaping about swinging wildly at the escaping rats with sticks of all shapes and sizes. Seeing the way things were likely to go, I left the arena and took a post outside, as did everybody else except Grandfather, who proceeded to dig, swing, chop, dance, curse and swear. After things had quietened down and all the rats had left, we took stock. The wire fence was completely demolished, six pullets were dead or dying and all the rats had escaped. I fell off my bike twice on the way home for I could not stop laughing. Rats produce the most extraordinary reactions from normally sane people.

One advantage with hunting rats is that there is little trouble finding somewhere to have a go. Most areas have large pieces of waste ground, even in the city areas, where rats abound. I know of about a dozen quite reasonable rat colonies within a mile of my home; not one of them is disturbed by anyone other than myself. Local authorities are hard-pressed these days to keep their spending down, so it is unlikely that they are going to spend time and money looking for rats unless they are prompted by a complaint from a taxpayer. Rats in open areas or empty buildings are left much to their own devices, and they are almost totally ignored on rubbish dumps. Consequently, a quick survey can produce quite a bit of free sport. Dogs again come into their own, for once a dog has developed a nose for rats it will never bypass them. It can be quite embarrassing when you are walking sedately down a quiet suburban street with your sweet little terrier nicely to heel when she suddenly leaps into a bush and emerges with a large rat. The first time my terrier bitch did this to me was in a very crowded street and it caused a terrible fuss. The trouble is that when the dog is attached to you by a lead, you can hardly disown the little darling.

Like rabbits, rats can be hunted with guns, dogs and hawks, but they are rarely netted. However, netting is a useful way of increasing the bag if you are single-handed or dogless. You can make miniature versions of standard purse nets with smaller meshes—one inch for preference—but a much simpler way of netting rats can be manufactured with empty tin cans and old socks. Cut both ends from a tin can and then push the resulting cylinder into the lower half of an old stocking, tucking the top inch or so inside the top of the tin and securing it with a couple of paper clips. All you then have to do is to push the tin into the entrance of the rat hole and, after entering your ferret, wait for the rat to rush through the tin only to come to a halt as it reaches the toe of the stocking. I have found that while stocking nets stop rats in their tracks quite effectively, they tend not to hold them for very long. You need to give the rat a clout with your stick as soon as it arrives.

When you have finished your day's ferreting, for rat or rabbit, don't forget to check your ferrets over for any damage before you put them away for the journey home. Clean any rabbit fleck from their feet and check their claws for injury while you are at it. Although the ferrets will usually be unharmed, even rabbits can inflict damage at times. A small wound left untreated can cause unnecessary suffering and possibly the death of a valuable member of your team. Having made sure that all is well, give them a drink. Then, if the pubs are still open—have one yourself.

Net
S I X **Making**

Since learning how to make my own nets, I have taught many people the art of net-making. Up until now the pupils have stood beside me and watched; I did once teach someone over the telephone, but this is the first time I have tried to write down the very simple technique.

The equipment you need is very basic. Many suppliers will sell you a complete net-making kit which includes the needle, wooden mesh-measure and all the twine, rings and drawline. Having obtained your materials, take the twine, load it onto your needle and tie the end of the twine to the first metal ring. Following the instructions shown in sketches 1 and 2, make the knots up to a number which suits your requirements for the width of the net. A purse net is usually 16 or 18 meshes wide. This method fixes the net to the rings in such a way as to make the whole thing firm.

When this first row has been completed, remove the wooden measure, which should be held tightly by the twine, and start the second row, making the knots as shown in sketch 3. This second row is made using the simple fisherman's knot, as are all the succeeding rows until you have 18 rows of mesh. It is a matter of personal preference just how long you make your nets, but 18 rows of two-inch mesh make a net which is conveniently one yard long and more than adequate for most situations. I do, however, have a few which are 24 rows long for use in large holes.

As each row is completed it should be pulled off the wooden measure and then, when you start the next row, taken up again, working from left to right. When you have completed the last row, leave it on the wooden measure and fix a new ring to your supporting hook as shown in sketch 1. Bring up the last row and tie the twine to the ring close against the bottom of the measure. Once you have done this, you may dispense with the measure and proceed to knit each loop onto the ring in the same style as at the start. When you come to the last loop, tie it off with a double knot as close to the ring as you can get and then cut the cord. This should leave you with a first-class net fitted with rings which are an integral rather than an additional part of the whole.

All the knots should be made firmly with tension on the twine, but not so much as to break it. Knots will slip unless you pull them tight, and you can be sure that the one that slips is the one which the rabbit hits. Having completed the net, it only remains for you to add the drawline and then finally to attach your wooden peg.

If you have been clever enough to follow these instructions you will soon be making nets which are just as good as—if not better than—any you can buy and much cheaper, too. The first net is difficult and you will probably make many mistakes. You will almost certainly miss a mesh here and there, only to discover it when you have finished a row; if you do, you will have to unpick the whole row until you get back to the mistake. After three nets you should have the hang of it; five will make you over-confident and you will start to makes mistakes again. Mistakes teach you to take care, for unpicking knots is hard on the fingers. After you have made eight or ten nets the whole thing will become automatic and you will be able to make them like a veteran. With a loop of string over your foot to tie your top ring to, you will be able to sit and make nets and watch television at the same

An occasional bone helps the ferret keep its 38 teeth trim.

time. It's just like knitting really, only easier as the stitches do not alter.

Once you have mastered hemp nets you can think of trying other materials, nylon being the usual choice. If you make nets with nylon you must make every knot in the net twice to stop it from slipping. Slipping knots are the bane of your life—the tension must be right when the knot is made or the net will be useless. Washing your nets and dyeing them before use does help to tighten them a little, but a loose knot is always a loose knot. If you can get it, rayon twine makes very good nets and doesn't need double-knotting. To start with you may find it difficult to handle, as it tends to skate about on the rings, but once you have mastered the art of making hemp nets you can soon overcome the initial problems of the synthetic twine. Rayon has the non-rotting advantages of nylon with the free-falling advantages of hemp and is well worth using.

You may like to experiment with your new-found skills and try making other nets. Fox nets, for example, should be six feet long with three-inch mesh. They are the same in all other respects. Rat nets can be produced with one-inch mesh as already mentioned. You may also like to turn out some longer nets about 4 to 12 yards long for ditches, gates and odd corners, but I would not advise you to try making a really long net. To make a 100-yard-long net you would have to make the equivalent of 150 purse nets; since a net is reduced in length by one-third when it is set, you would be better off making the 150 purse nets. If you decide to make a long net from hemp, remember it will weigh over ten pounds when dry, and if you get it wet it will weigh an awful lot more; in addition you will have to find somewhere to dry it properly or it will rot and your weeks of patient work will have been wasted. It is much better to buy a long nylon net—currently it is also cheaper.

BEGINNING STAGES IN MAKING YOUR OWN FERRETING NETS

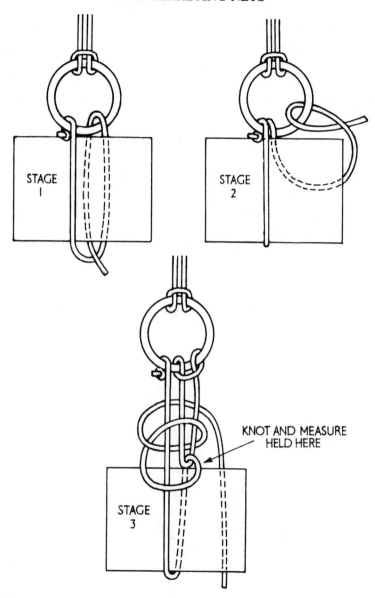

KNOT AND MEASURE
HELD HERE

STAGE 1

STAGE 2

STAGE 3

Nets can be quite costly. You may choose to make your own nets; if so, this diagram shows you how to get started.

A final word on nets. The wooden pegs that you buy are made of ash and are long-lasting and quite convenient, with a wide top to prevent them falling through the rings in the net and causing trouble, but they seem quite costly. I make pegs from pieces of hazel or chestnut around six inches long with a point at one end and a groove at the other to hold the drawline. They do occasionally fall through the top ring, but as each of the nets is held in place by an elastic band when not in use that problem is minimal. The pegs cost nothing—most of them are cut from a hazel tree growing beside my ferret pens. I would need to spend about £15 ($30) to buy ash pegs for my stock of nets. With that money I could buy enough hemp twine and drawline to make another 45 nets. I know which I would rather have.

Ferreting and the Law

Whichever method of ferreting you come to favor, there is one thing you must have—the right to be on the land where you practice your art.* Too many people believe that they can go on any land that takes their fancy and catch any rabbits they see hopping around: "It's only a few old bunnies for the pot, guv'nor." But, while rabbit poaching has never been a hanging offense, it has always been an offense to some degree. All land is owned by someone. Without going too deeply into the game laws and their strictures, you can be pretty certain that those rabbits come under someone's protection and are not yours for the taking. Rabbits are specifically mentioned in most of the laws referring to game. They occupy a peculiar place—they are vermin but they are also ground game. Although rabbits, along with other game, cannot (in most instances) be classed as the property of any individual while they are alive, they become the property of the landowner on whose land they lie once they are dead.

*The reader should remember that this chapter applies only to Great Britain. Be sure to be familiar with the laws of your state before attempting to hunt any animal with ferrets.

To cast aside any doubt you may have about the poaching of rabbits, let me quote from *Stone's Justices' Manual*: "Poaching is the offence committed by a person who pursues, kills, or takes certain game birds and animals on land where he has no right to go." Deliberately trying to go no farther than the average person wanting to find out his rights on common land, I called at a number of police stations in my own area, which has many large chunks of common heathland holding small populations of rabbits. I was told by each desk sergeant I met that he could find no entry telling him that I was not allowed to take rabbits on common land, and that if I wished to check further I would need to look up the relevant cases, which would take a very long time. What all these kindly policemen did say was that, in practice, most areas of common land are looked after by either the county council or a common-preservation society and that those bodies would, no doubt, employ a legal mind to find some offense to prosecute you with. The police, it seems, are more likely to turn a blind eye or just tell you to push off.

In their efforts to find any offense, it was noticeable that all these policemen failed to look up the local bylaws. On most entrances to common land you will find a notice referring to the National Parks and Access to the Countryside Act, 1949, which provides for your county council to pass bylaws governing the rights of access and the activities you may indulge in, usually on specific pieces of land. Among other things, you are prohibited from setting traps, snares or nets or catching wild animals without permission. You will see therefore that things are pretty well tied up all around, and even on the common land not mentioned in the local bylaws you will find you need permission to take rabbits.

While in many areas the police may turn a blind eye to rabbiting activities on common land, owners of private land are less tolerant. In the last few years landowners

THE WORLD'S LARGEST SELECTION OF PET, ANIMAL, AND MUSIC BOOKS.

T.F.H. Publications publishes more than 900 books covering many hobby aspects (dogs, cats, birds, fish, small animals, music, etc.). Whether you are a beginner or an advanced hobbyist you will find exactly what you're looking for among our complete listing of books. For a free catalog fill out the form on the other side of this page and mail it today.

. . CATS . . .

. . . BIRDS . .

. . . ANIMALS . . .

. . . DOGS . . .

. . FISH . . .

. . . MUSIC . . .

For more than 30 years, *Tropical Fish Hobbyist* has been the source of accurate, up-to-the-minute, and fascinating information on every facet of the aquarium hobby.

Join the more than 50,000 devoted readers worldwide who wouldn't miss a single issue.

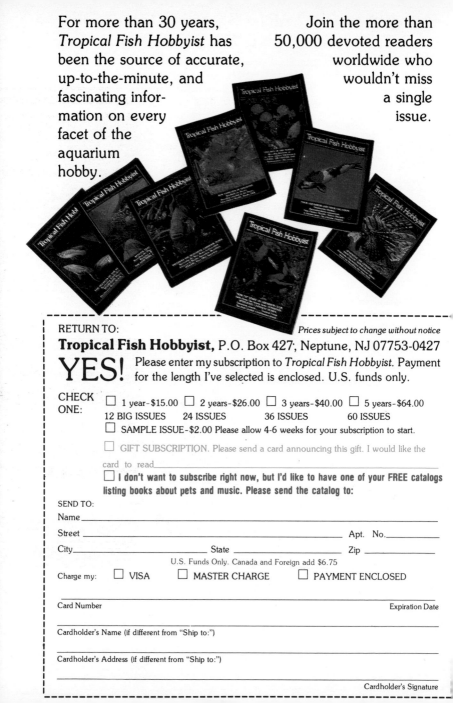

with sporting rights and sporting tenants have been faced with escalating costs, coupled with increased poaching of all kinds. Added to the seasonal poaching of game-birds by organized gangs is the huge rise in the "lamping" of rabbits, hares, foxes and deer with running dogs. Although most shoots are pleased to see the back of any fox, it is hardly surprising that, faced with these incursions, landowners are becoming less likely to let someone off with a warning. With the rise in the number of prosecutions comes a hardening of attitudes on the part of the courts, which are now dealing with offenders much more severely. Two men were recently fined £20 plus £25 costs (about $90 total) each at Romsey in Hampshire for the taking of one rabbit with ferrets.

Ferreting must be the least effective form of poaching and the most vulnerable to discovery. If you have a ferret to ground and a whole series of purse nets laid out, it is difficult to run off and impossible to deny what you are about! It is not like running a dog during the day, when at least you can say that you are only out for a walk and the dog does not belong to you. The old Gypsies used to train their dogs to stay back when a stranger came up, and the dogs were often working on reversed instructions—"Come here, boy" meant "Go away," for example. You can hardly do that with ferrets—they usually go away anyway!

You do not have to be standing on enclosed land to attract the attention of the police, for they have the power to stop and search anyone they have good reason to suspect is coming from land where he may have been in pursuit of game. Note the word *may*, for you need not even have been successful. They also have the power to seize any article you may be carrying, including guns, nets, traps, snares, etc. I suppose it is some consolation to learn that they do not have the power to seize your dogs or your ferrets. While the police may not be overly interested in your efforts on common land, they are much more interested when you poach private land. The offense is easier to find for a start, and very often if a shoot is involved the local bobby is a member of the beating team and you are spoiling his personal sport as well.

POACHING FOR EXCITEMENT

Why do people poach rabbits in the first place? I think that most poaching is done by men who have no legitimate place to hunt. Most newcomers to the sport have their ferrets before they have anywhere to use them, as is proved by the numbers who ask the organized societies for help in finding somewhere. The Ferret Society is constantly being asked to provide ferreting for newcomers (it does not do so). Similarly, the Wildfowler's Association of Great Britain and Ireland is frequently asked to find sport for members; again it cannot do so, as a rule. In addition, a few people poach the odd rabbit out of a mixture of devilment and sport—certainly not for money, as the costs of keeping ferrets and getting to where the rabbits are far outweigh the value of the bag.

Regrettably, worthwhile ferreting is hard to come by, particularly in the Home Counties. Because of the costs of running even a small shoot today, rabbits are not only part of the bag, but often a very important part. Many people are prepared to pay high prices for the chance to work a parcel of land. Advertisements throughout the year in the sporting press ask for ferreting, rough-shooting or simple vermin-shooting opportunities. Useful replies are rare. As a result there are few ferreting men— apart from those brought up in the game and those brought up on land—who can truthfully say that they have never gone in for just a *little* bit of poaching. I am lucky in no longer needing to poach rabbits in order to exercise my ferrets. But then, I have worked hard for my ferreting, and some of the ground I can use has been negotiated over many years. For one piece in particular, I was seeking permission for 12 years on and off; having given up all hope of ever getting it, out of the blue I was *asked* to clear the rabbits. Quite apart from legal considerations, it is much easier to keep in touch with the action when you do not have to keep looking over your shoulder.

Undoubtedly some people occasionally enjoy the excitement of a little bit of illicit ferreting. On one memorable occasion my daughter and I set out before dawn on what promised to be a beauitful mid-August morning in order to bolt a few rabbits from a piece of ground that was jumping with them; the rabbits could be numbered in hundreds in each hedgerow. In common with most poachers I had few nets, 18 to be precise, and the burrows were so full of holes it was a wonder the trees in the hedges didn't fall over. We arrived on the ground at 3:30 a.m., just as the light was beginning to show. The fields were waist-high in morning mist, and as we knelt down to set our pathetically few nets, we must have been totally invisible to anyone who chanced to look, although at that hour we were unlikely to be disturbed. Once the nets were down we entered the ferrets, one jill and her two ten-week-old kits. Within seconds rabbits started bolting in all directions. The hedgerow we had chosen to start on was all of 200 yards long, and we had set the 18 nets in the middle. For every rabbit that hit them we must have lost at least ten. I have never seen anything like it before or since. After about ten minutes everything went quiet again and we retrieved the ferrets. All this action had been caused almost single-handedly by the adult jill, as her kits had only puttered in and out, playing games with each other. We picked up our nets and moved on to the next hedge, where the same thing happened all over again, and again and again.

Getting carried away with the excitement of it all, we failed to watch the time, and before we knew it, it was 5:30 a.m. I was sitting in a dry ditch, removing a rabbit from a

True polecats (such as the ones depicted in this drawing by art-ist/naturalist Michael Clark) are wild and free and therefore exhibit a different behavior from domestic polecat/ferrets which are sold as pets.

net—with my intrepid daughter doing the same thing on the other side of the hedge—when to my horror I saw a man creeping toward me across the field with a twelve-gauge shotgun pointed straight at me. He was dressed in a short dressing-gown and slippers, nothing else. After a whispered conversation, we two poachers melted into the ground. Suddenly the gunman changed direction and I realized that he was not stalking me but was himself after rabbits, too. His bold approach and his dressing-gown indicated that he had more right to be there than we had. My ferret box was on the path in full view, and the mist was by now not nearly thick enough to give me cover if I moved to retrieve it. I just had to sit there and hope he would go through the gate into the next field and give us the chance to slip away, but he did not. Instead, he followed the hedge down the path toward me, and such was his concentration that he nearly fell over my box. "Good morning. Dressed for the part I see," I said as brightly as I could muster, with the private thought that satirical comments like that would get me hung one day. The poor man was so surprised by my sudden appearance that he nearly shot his foot off. This, coupled with the voice of my daughter saying "Hallo" from the other side of the hedge and the fact he was only wearing a dressing-gown (remember, I was sitting in a ditch) unsettled him a bit. He muttered something about not minding us taking a few rabbits but not to make a habit of it and not to let the keeper catch us at it, and left us to clear off with our booty. I cannot recall exactly how many rabbits we caught that morning, but I know I was sitting on seven when he came up.

I never went back to that land again, having had a fair and decent warning, although I used to peer wistfully over the fence once in a while. Shortly afterward I heard that all the hedges in that ground had been gassed, a terrible waste from a ferreter's point of view. I blame myself entirely; if I had gone about things in the right way and asked, I might have had the chance to have had a really good go at that multitude of rabbits. The numbers have never come back as the use of the ground has changed, so I will never know.

FINDING GOOD GROUND

In spite of the undoubted excitement of poaching, however, the average ferreter would much prefer to work his animals legitimately. Perhaps the best advice I can offer the would-be ferreter—apart from the obvious "first find your ferreting"—is to get to know the right people. With any sport or pastime it seems to be a case of who you know, rather than what you know. If you have gone the rounds of the local farms without success and you are still game to try, then get yourself involved with field sports and the countryside in general. Join the foot followers of the hunt and get to know some of the people. Even better, join the Ferret Society or perhaps the local branch of the Young Farmers' Club—you do not need to be a young farmer, and you may meet someone who can help. If you get the chance on even the smallest bit of ground, do the job properly. Be seen to be correct in all that you do. Above all, don't just do the easy bits—more ferreting is lost to the gasman that way—and do check on your boundaries.

As recently as last season I was made to look stupid when about to ferret a small area of woodland. The landowner had walked me around the property in the summer, showing me where he thought the rabbits were and pointing out the boundaries. He made mention of a fence-line above a hanging wood which was his top boundary, but we did not go and look at it. I went over one wet November morning with two friends I had invited along in return for a similar trip to their ground. We were about to start laying nets when a party of five or six men hove into view and their leader asked me, fairly politely in the circumstances, just what I thought I was up to. It transpired, much to my embarrassment, that I was faced with the true owner of the land on which I was standing, and to make matters worse, he was about to ferret that particular burrow. The boundary fence I ought to have been working to was a long-since collapsed fence some 50 yards down the hill. There were a lot of rabbits about, but few were actually on the land owned by my man. The damage they were causing to his vegetables was enough for him to want to be rid of them at any price. I apologized and backed out as gracefully as I could, much to the amusement of my two friends. In the end we did manage to catch one rabbit that morning, or rather the dog did. The only rabbit we bolted slipped the net and was picked up by my whippet, who had spent the morning complaining that she was cold and wet and there was nothing for her to do. At least she cheered up.

In Sickness and
Health—Ailments

When you take on the ownership of any caged creature, you suddenly become endowed with the powers of life and death. You make all its decisions for it: what it eats and drinks, when it eats, when it mates and how often and when it dies. The owner of livestock must be aware of his or her responsibilities. It is up to you to see that your ferrets never encounter the avoidable sicknesses and to at least try to help if they are struck down by the unavoidable.

Ferrets are strong and healthy animals with no great tendency to become sick, but the nature of their work and the food they eat make them liable to a few conditions not common to all small animals. Few ferreters keep sufficient numbers of animals to become experts at diagnosis; most of us are unlikely to have much experience with anything other than the simple ailments and some of the classic diseases. But contrary to popular opinion among ferreters, many veterinary surgeons today are well-versed in the major afflictions of ferrets—not as many as I would like, but because of the increase of interest in the subject, many more vets are being presented with ferrets at their surgeries. My own vets are very good, and while they never claim any special knowledge, I have on more than one occasion had cause to be grateful to them. Added to this, quite a number of vets are themselves keeping working ferrets.

To ensure good health, it is important to raise your pet under clean, dry conditions. Despite your proper care and handling, ferrets may contract diseases from the food they eat or from contact with infected quarry such as rabbits or rats.

There is a basic veterinary problem with ferrets, as with many small mammals, which is difficult to overcome. They tend to show very similar symptoms (or clinical signs, as vets now call them) for a multitude of ills, which makes diagnosis hard even for the experts. They also have the disconcerting ability to mask all the symptoms of their illness until they are poised at death's door. By the time you find out that you have a sick ferret it is often too late to do anything about it. You should therefore be on your guard and pay attention to any behavior which appears out of the ordinary. If your ferret goes off its food, fluffs up and refuses to leave its bed, then it is obviously sick; but if you have your wits about you, you will notice its loss of zest before it reaches this stage and do something about it. The rule of thumb ought to be "Prevention is better than cure"—it is cheaper, too, in terms of both cash and of ferrets' lives.

If you are going to maintain healthy ferrets, you must give them clean, dry conditions. When you keep only small numbers your stock often stays free of disease, but when you increase your numbers you also increase the likelihood of infection. If you have ever read a veterinary manual on any one animal species it can put you right off that species for life. As a practical stockman, not a veterinary surgeon, I can here give you some idea of what the possible problems are and what can be done to alleviate them. Some you can obviously deal with yourself, and this chapter tries to show the approach; but a few, even at first sight, are beyond your help. Beyond this, the best advice is to get your animal to a vet, where at least it has a chance of a cure. All too often the cost of taking a working ferret to the vet is far more than the cost of replacement, so the animal is put down. But the modern vet is frequently presented with sick ferrets—and surely a working animal is entitled to this much and more. If you have no intention of seeking qualified advice, at least put the animal down quickly and painlessly.

According to old-time ferreters there are only two diseases suffered by ferrets—the *sweats* and the *staggers*. In reality these names cover a number of conditions, some of which are fatal, some merely irritating. Recently a group of men told me that they would never go to a vet and never considered trying to save any ferret which showed signs of weakness or ill-health; they would simply destroy the affected animal and there was an end to it. These rather harsh measures undoubtedly help to keep stock disease-free, but they also result in the unnecessary death of good animals. To illustrate their point they brought along a ferret which they believed to be suffering from the staggers. As luck would have it, I was able to show them that it was in fact suffering only from mites in the ears and could tell them a simple and effective cure. This served to show that at least owners should take time to check before simply destroying out of hand.

CUTS, ABRASIONS AND BITES

Because of the nature of a ferret's work, cuts and abrasions frequently occur, as do bites. If dealt with right away, they can be classed as little more than a nuisance. If left alone, they can become more serious. Ferrets working in rubbish dumps can often cut themselves on broken glass or rusty tins; they can also cut themselves in the confines of their own cage if you leave any sharp edges or projecting nails. They may be bitten by rats, knocked about by large rabbits or even hurt by each other. The latter does not happen too often among a group of jills, but if you are foolish enough to leave a group of hobs together in the spring, the damage can be very serious indeed.

Wash small cuts with a mild antiseptic (and I mean mild), clip the hair away from the site if necessary and apply a good antiseptic powder or ointment. If a cut bleeds freely it usually heals quickly and well, since the body's natural healing agents cleanse the tissues. I have often found that really bad injuries mend faster than small ones, particularly when profuse bleeding has occurred. But remember that large cuts may need a stitch or two. If the wound is slowly welling blood, it is likely to be a deep one and therefore difficult to clean. Not only that, but there may be other complications and perhaps internal damage.

Deeper wounds and bites will often benefit from antibiotic treatment, particularly rat bites, which carry some real "nasties" passed on in the rat's saliva. The classic is *rat-bite fever*, which you too can get if bitten. It is characterized by swellings under the arms or in the groin area on the side nearest the bite and also by swelling at the site of the infection. I have heard of one old countryman who always carried a bottle of friar's balsam when out ferreting rats. If a ferret was bitten he applied the balsam directly to the bite and claimed never to have had a case of rat-bite fever. He also used it to guard young ferrets against distemper, painting their noses with it if an infected dog had been in contact with his stock. He never lost any ferrets from distemper, and this was at a time when the disease was prevalent! But I have no direct experience with this treatment and therefore cannot comment except to say that the man in question hunted a lot of rats. I would recommend that in the event of bites you seek a good antibiotic treatment.

FLEAS, TICKS AND LICE

Everyone knows what a flea looks like and most of us have seen a tick or two, but the younger reader may never have seen lice. Ticks are the fat brownish creatures with their heads buried in the skin of your animal. They vary in size depending on the amount of food they have taken, but they can sometimes be as large as the nail on your little finger. Lice are generally smaller and pear-shaped; lice can be pulled off intact and ticks cannot. Working ferrets will often come home with rabbit fleas, and they may also pick up fleas from their hay or straw bedding, particularly in the summer. Ticks will almost certainly find their way onto your ferrets if they are worked in an area where sheep predominate. Lice are not very common by comparison, and I have only once come across them on my ferrets. On that occasion I had been ferreting rats from under a shed and they had found a particularly lousy resident hedgehog.

Fleas and lice can be dealt with quickly and effectively with one or other of the many powders, aerosol sprays or insecticidal shampoos readily available from any pet shop. Naturally care should be taken when using sprays around the face of an affected animal, and if you are dealing with parasites on a nursing jill, I suggest that you leave her with her lodgers until she has reared her family and then de-flea the whole lot. Ferrets, unlike cats, do not seem to object to being sprayed with insecticide. Always follow the instructions on the container and do not forget to change the bedding and treat the cage as well, or you will be back to square one in no time at all.

Ticks are a different matter as they do not respond to flea powders or sprays. Some people tell you to use the end of a lighted cigarette to deal with them: you need a very steady hand to be able to deal with a tick like this, as it could result in a branded ferret and a bitten hand. There are much simpler ways of dealing with ticks, which should please the non-smokers! One thing you *should not* do is pull them off, as they can leave their mouthparts embedded in the ferret's flesh and cause an abscess or a sore. Treatment depends on where the tick is located. If it is on the face, paint kerosene or household flyspray on the tick with an artist's brush. The tick should drop off within 24 hours, but if it persists just repeat the process. Ticks on the body can be treated with a burst of flyspray, which should be rubbed into the fur to ensure penetration to any hidden away. When using flyspray, hold it close to the affected part. Some petshops now stock a very effective product produced specifically for ticks. Remember that sprays designed for use on fleas have little effect on ticks.

WORMS

Like every other creature, ferrets on occasion suffer from worms. Rabbits often have tapeworms in their gut, and these may be passed on to ferrets when they are fed rabbit if you do not check the carcass. Fortunately, these worms can now be dealt with effectively by one of the many simple worm treatments on the market for dogs and cats. However, because of the small body weight of the average ferret it is often best to seek veterinary advice on the average dosage. In time there may be a worm treatment made specifically for ferrets, as I was recently asked for an opinion on the subject by a manufacturer of these medicines.

The first signs of worms in a ferret or any other animal are usually a voracious appetite coupled with loss of weight—the animal is thin, active, rough-coated and always hungry. Sometimes though, the first indication will be segments in the droppings. It does no harm to make a regular practice of worming your stock, just to be sure. Many ferreters believe that rabbit fur keeps worms at bay. I feed my ferrets rabbit portions with the skin on occasionally, and it is true that I have never had worms in my stock, but that may well be a coincidence. Foxes eat rabbit skins and they get worms! *Do not* go shoving powdered glass or chewing tobacco down the unfortunate animal's throat: these devilish treatments were often advised by the old school of ferreters.

MITES

Mites come in many varieties and afflict ferrets in several ways; none are very pleasant, but all are curable if treated properly.

Mange Mites

Mange is probably the most common problem caused

by mites; also, it can be passed on to you. There are several types of mange mites, and they can be extremely difficult to get rid of; they are also, from the layman's point of view, difficult to identify. The sarcoptic mange mite is the one most likely to turn up if you feed your stock on wild rodents and foxes, and I have already recommended that you do not do this. But your ferrets can also pick up the mites from infected ground, so you must be prepared to deal with it.

The first sign of mange is that the animal is incessantly scratching. To begin with you may find nothing and may even treat your animal for fleas, but as the mange progresses the skin will become red and sore; this is particularly obvious in white ferrets. Following this, bald patches covered with red blotches and sores start to appear. The simplest treatment is to cover the animal in benzyl benzoate, which you may be able to obtain from your druggist or veterinarian. Benzyl benzoate is a thin cream which blocks all the pores, so you must not cover the animal all at once. Do half the animal at a time—half one day and half the next. Apply the cream, leave it for 24 hours, wash it off, and then apply cream to the second half. Leave it again for 24 hours and then wash it off. This treatment should be repeated again in 48 hours. You should, of course, clean the cage thoroughly and leave the affected animal in a fresh cage or box during the treatment. With any mite infection I recommend that you use a blowtorch to clean the cage and then repaint it.

Ear Mites

A simple infection with the mite *Otodectes cyanotis* can give a ferret untold hours of discomfort and misery. Ear mites should be suspected if your animal spends much of its time scratching its ears. On looking into the ears you will find quite a lot of wax and a number of black specks. These specks are the colonies of mites. If left untreated they cause the ferret to scratch its ears until they bleed.

Occasionally the mites move down into the middle ear and set up an infection known as *middle-ear disease*—this is what had happened to the ferret with "the staggers" that I mentioned earlier. I never saw this ferret—nor one of my own jills which became infected—scratch once. My jill first showed signs of being in trouble when she started to stagger about. As the problem progressed (over a period of a few hours) she began to drag herself around, using only her front legs and towing her hindquarters uselessly behind. A veterinarian friend and I spent some time watching her stagger round his living room one Sunday evening before he thought of examining her ears and found the tell-tale signs of mites. A twice-daily application of drops directly into the ears for ten days will cure this problem very simply. It is also important to treat any other animals which have been in contact with the infected animal, whether they show the symptoms or not. This is a classic example of how one disease can exhibit the characteristics of another and more serious disease and shows that care must be taken with diagnosis.

Foot Rot

It used to be thought that foot rot was caused by wet and filthy cages, but while it is true that these do aggravate the condition, they are not the actual cause. Foot rot is a mite-based ailment that is particularly unpleasant—the feet swell, become scabby and eventually lose their claws. If it is not dealt with right away the feet can be literally eaten away. It is an understatement to say that it causes the poor ferret considerable pain, and it is surely a very unfeeling owner who allows his animal to get into this state.

Isolate infected animals and then examine their companions carefully and remove them to clean quarters. Burn the bedding where it is with a blowtorch and wash the cages very thoroughly with a strong hot solution of washing soda. Soak the feet of the animal in warm soapy water, then remove the scabs and cut the claws back. Make sure that the scabs are well-soaked before removing them, as they will then come off more easily. Either way your ferret is unlikely to take kindly to this treatment and is sure to let you know about it. If you do get bitten, blame yourself, as you should never have let it reach this stage. After the feet have been cleaned and dried, apply sulphur ointment or benzyl benzoate until the condition has cleared up. I am happy to say that cases of foot rot are now somewhat rarer than they once were.

It is very important to check that your breeding ferrets are free from all these parasites *before* mating. It is not advisable to treat a jill for fleas, lice, ticks or mites during the later stages of her pregnancy or while nursing young, as most of the products used to kill skin parasites will also kill off young ferrets.

GROWTHS AND LUMPS

These fall into two catagories—*abscesses* and *tumors*. Abscesses are fairly common in ferrets and arise from several causes, including bites and unclean wounds. The appearance of an abscess can be very sudden, and although they frequently do not seem to worry the ferret, they certainly worry the owner. Neck and throat abscesses are usually caused by mucosal damage, damage to the salivary ducts due to swallowing small spicules of bone or even to dental problems. Such abscesses often reach the size of a golf ball and can seriously interfere with feeding. There are basically two types of abscesses—one caused by infection, the other by obstruction—and both are filled with fluid which can be pressed from one side to the other. A simply way of proving an abscess is to shine a strong pencil flashlight onto one part of the swelling in a darkened room; the whole mass will glow as the light passes through the fluid. Any abscess needs to be drained of its pus and treated with a suitable antibiotic. This is, of course, a job for a vet, and if the abscess is caused by an obstruction in the salivary duct, this must also be cleared.

Tumors are usually much slower-growing than an abscess and are very hard to the touch. They can be cancerous or non-malignant. For a cancerous tumor there is rarely any treatment, and the vet is likely to recommend that the animal be destroyed. A non-malignant tumor can be removed by surgery, but if it is in the area of the throat its removal can be so complex that few vets would consider their chances very high.

PROBLEMS WITH JILLS

Some of the problems that can affect jill ferrets have been mentioned in the chapter on breeding, but here they will be considered more fully. Jill ferrets, like any other females, have specific problems which can lead to their deaths. As already stated, I do not hold the widespread belief tht a jill will die unless she has been mated by her second season; I have yet to be shown any clinical evidence to support this theory. It is, however, a fact that unmated jills do sometimes fade away and die. Such deaths can be traced on many occasions to infections of the womb. These can be caused by the entry of dirt and bacteria through the enlarged vulva when the animals are in heat. There is no doubt that they are very vulnerable in this condition, and you should therefore take extra care that they are kept clean. During a prolonged period of estrus they tend to lose weight and condition, and if this happens they can become vulnerable to any disease which may be going the rounds. If jills die, it is not because they have not been to the hob. If they are becoming sick it is up to you to take action—don't just sit there worrying about old tales.

Mated jills may die, too. Any mated jill has to run the risk of abortion, womb infections and fetal death during the course of pregnancy, followed by parturition problems, hemorrhage and milk fever after the birth of her kits. All in all, I think the unmated jill stands a better chance! A jill who has recently delivered kits should be swift on her feet, trim and neat, and very alert. If she is not, there is something wrong. Frequently a jill will not like being picked up when she has a new family, but if she is looking below par you *must* check her over. If she is suffering from a hemorrhage there is little you can do for her and she will become progressively weaker until she dies. It may be that she has a kit stuck in the birth canal, in which case a vet can help. Womb infections such as *metritis* can be dealt with by administration of suitable antibiotics. Most often, though, the reason for the jill's ill-health is milk fever, which is caused by the drain on her calcium reserves. She will start to show signs of this about a week following the birth. In cattle, milk fever is referred to as "the staggers," and it is well-named. The jill will hump her back up, look both listless and thin and will waver on her feet like a drunk. She is in urgent need of a large dose of calcium, which must be injected into her quickly. In any case of post-natal sickness, you must get your animal to the vet as soon as possible if you are to save her and her family.

HEAT EXHAUSTION

Heat exhaustion is one of the conditions referred to as "the sweats," with some justification. It is caused by too much heat, aggravated by poorly ventilated boxes, stuffy cages and bad placement of the quarters. Many animals die from it every year, particularly in mid-summer. If you find an animal dead in its cage on a hot day and its cage is in the full sun, you may well have a case of heat exhaustion. Avoid a cage position which takes the full force of the midday sun and make sure that there is adequate ventilation; if some sun must inevitably reach the cage, cover the roof with a dampened sack on hot days.

It is not just at home that heat exhaustion can strike. The only case I have had was on a very warm November afternoon when I inadvertently left one of my favorite jills in the full sun while I was setting nets. After about an hour I went to take her from her box and found her in a collapsed state. At first I thought she was dead, but after I had rolled her in the damp grass for a few minutes she recovered and went on to bolt a few rabbits for me later in the day.

Overheating and heat exhaustion can happen very quickly. A friend of mine lost a whole family of ferrets as the result of a 30 minute car journey on a hot afternoon. His ferrets were in a well-ventilated traveling box on the back seat of his car, when he found himself stuck in a traffic jam. In spite of the fact that all his windows were open, the ferrets all died; there simply was not enough air movement to cool them down. Be wary of small traveling boxes (however well-ventilated) in hot weather. I heard that a large number of ferrets died in their boxes at a game fair one year because of this problem; the animals I had on display myself at that show were very hot and sticky, in spite of being out of the sun and in all-wire display pens. I was very aware of the problem and kept them cool with a water spray during the worst part of the day. Such is the problem that at another show I spent a considerable amount of time reviving ferrets that were brought to me suffering from the heat, and the organizer of the ferret fair—Pugs and Drummers—is considering discontinuing the sale of ferrets during its first two days because the new owners will insist on carrying their purchases around in small boxes in the full sun.

If you find any ferret in a collapsed state on a hot day, you can be fairly certain that you will have a dead animal on your hands unless you act quickly. Immerse the sufferer in a bowl of cool water or, if you are out in the fields, try the grass on the shady side of a hedge. Most animals will soon recover if caught in time and cooled down rapidly. They should then be allowed a rest and a drink in a cool place.

Having dealt with most of the simpler problems, we now come to the viral and bacterial infections which can occasionally beset the ferret.

INFLUENZA

There are many strains of flu virus, and most are very infectious. I remember as a young soldier in a training unit being one of about 30 men left on their feet out of a unit of over a thousand! All the strains produce similar and easily recognizable symptoms which are the same for your ferrets as they are for you.

It is well known that ferrets are very susceptible to respiratory troubles, and although they should not die from a mild case of flu if properly nursed and kept warm, they will succumb to pneumonia if that follows it. Dry draft-free quarters (which should be given to ferrets as a matter of course) will go a long way toward preventing flu, and if you are suffering from flu yourself you should keep away from your stock and get someone else to deal with them until you are clear. Ferrets are used as a research animal by many laboratories involved in the production of flu vaccines, and you can be sure they would not waste their time with animals which were not susceptible to the virus they are working with. Do not dismiss flu as just another minor illness. Its complications can and will kill if not treated.

TUBERCULOSIS

As few ferrets are submitted for post-mortem examination, and as this is usually the only way that tuberculosis can be diagnosed, no one can be sure how many ferrets die from it. In the event of the condition being discovered before death there is little that can be done. Occasionally tumors are found to be tuberculous. The best course is to have the animal destroyed. Ferrets are susceptible to bovine, human and avian tuberculosis, and although most dairy herds are now free from it and human tuberculosis is rare, there is still the danger of avian tuberculosis, as already mentioned in the chapter on feeding.

LEPTOSPIROSIS

Sometimes referred to as *Weil's disease* or *ratcatcher's jaundice*, leptospirosis can kill humans. If you hunt rats with ferrets and dogs you place yourself, your ferrets and your dogs in considerable danger. It is not enough just to make sure that you do not come into direct contact with rats by avoiding handling them; you must also ensure that you do not come into contact with their urine, either directly from the rats themselves—who will urinate with fear when caught—or indirectly from the ground on which they run, as that too may be carrying the infection. This applies particularly to any wet areas. There are often high concentrations of leptospires in the places where rats live. For example, the River Thames at Chertsey is heavily infected, as a friend of mine discovered when he had his stream (which runs directly into the main river) checked before setting up a fish-farming project. His children and my daughter used to ride their ponies into the stream and swim with them in hot weather. That stopped!

A few people have died in recent years as a result of hunting rats, in addition to a few deaths among farm workers (who contract Weil's disease while cutting wet vegetables in the fields) and a small number of bathers. If you feed infected rats to your ferrets, you run the risk of infection yourself, as it is just possible that they may pass it on to you. Up to 65% of wild rats can be infected in an average colony. The bacteria live in the rats' kidneys and are passed out on occasion in the urine. If they dry out they die, but if kept moist they will survive. I know of no cases where ferrets have passed on the infection, but there may be just the chance—the ferret may pick up the bacteria on its feet and pass it to you in this way. There does not need to be any break in the skin, as the bacteria can be absorbed through the skin.

I have a family to support, apart from which I enjoy life

very much; therefore I do not take too many chances when hunting rats. If you hunt rats, at least give your dogs and ferrets a fair chance and have them immunized.

ENTERITIS

Sometimes caused by feeding too much slop, enteritis can also be due to *Escherichia coli*. This bacterial infection of the gut, normally resident in most animals to some extent, can build up to a level which will cause the death of its host. Young ferrets recently out of the nest are the ones most likely to suffer. They become badly diarrhetic, lose water and rapidly die, probably as much from dehydration as from the *E. coli* bacteria. Adults do not seem to be affected to the same extent. In cases of enteritis it is advisable to reduce the amount of whole-carcass meat—remove the gut of any animal fed to the young stock and feed them on a proportion of pellet food. To control the condition use kaolin, given by mouth, as young kits have been found to respond to this very well.

SALMONELLA

Salmonella is a large group of bacteria associated with food poisoning, very often occurring in uncooked or improperly cooked chicken, and occasionally troubling ferrets. Nevertheless, ferrets seem to be very resistant to the salmonella bug, and few animals succumb.

DISTEMPER

Canine distemper is the old mystery killer and the disease most often referred to as "the sweats." Though much less of a danger now than formerly, it is still a great killer of ferrets. Affected animals suffer a discharge from the eyes and nose and have difficulty with breathing, to the extent that they cough and wheeze. They go on to suffer diarrhea, which is itself a weakener, and finally fall victim to fits. Sometimes they rally and appear to be over the worst, but all too often this is followed by a relapse from which they rarely recover.

There is no specific treatment except prior protection by inoculation. Over the years a considerable number of ferrets have been used in the search for and the production of a suitable vaccine to protect dogs against distemper. This vaccine will also protect your ferrets, and the dose normally given to one dog may be used for four ferrets. You may have to get your vet to order the right vaccine for you as not every one is suitable. Without this protection ferrets will die like flies if the infection reaches them, and the whole of your stock can be wiped out. Fortunately, as more and more dog-owners have their animals protected at an early age, the incidence of this killer disease is dropping. Nevertheless, contact with a newly purchased and sick puppy will all too often be found to be the cause of an outbreak. I regularly hear from people who have unwittingly caused the death of their entire stock of ferrets by introducing an unprotected dog into the immediate environment.

POST-NEST PARALYSIS

In recent years, I have heard of increasing numbers of young kits leaving the nest with their hindquarters paralyzed and the back legs operating like flippers. There seem to be three basic causes, all of which are dietary. If you take care with the diet and rear your young stock properly, the problem should never occur.

The first cause is *rickets*, which is due to a lack of vitamin D. It can be avoided by ensuring that your ferrets receive a balanced diet.

The second cause is a result of feeding a high proportion of liver and is known as *hypervitaminosis*. A high-liver diet causes an excessive build-up of vitamins, particularly vitamin A, rather than a shortage. This results in excessive bone formation at the hip and spinal joints. In some litters not all the kits are affected; it seems likely that since liver is a popular first choice with ferrets, those who repeatedly grabbed it first are the ones that

170

suffer. It is cured by injections of anabolic steroids which encourage rapid growth and burn up the excessive vitamins in the animal's body. Adult ferrets can also suffer, but the symptoms can take several years to show. Liver is often available in large quantities at reasonable prices, and when you are faced with a number of hungry kits you may well be tempted to feed them this to the exclusion of everything else. *Don't*. Adult ferrets can stand a diet of up to 90% liver and come to no harm, but youngsters cannot.

The third cause of post-nest paralysis which may be attributed to diet is *vitamin* **B** *(thiamine) deficiency*. It occurs when ferrets are fed on scraps containing fish which may have an antithiamine substance in them. Treatment consists of the administration of thiamine, either by mouth or by injection. Adult ferrets fed on table scraps may also be affected.

BOTULISM

I have deliberately taken this bacterial infection out of sequence and placed it at the end of my catalog of ills, for it is probably the biggest killer of ferrets. Strangely, I can find no mention of it in any literature or handbook of ferret management outside research laboratories. It is a well-known killer of mink, which are closely related, and on at least one occasion was shown to be the cause of the death of the entire stock of a small mink farm. (Small mink farms number their stock in hundreds rather than thousands.) During the winter of 1978-1979, I lost a great many good ferrets, including some of the best workers I am ever likely to own, through botulism.

Most of us have heard of it, perhaps through the news of recalls of cans of infected mushrooms or salmon that occur on occasion. We also hear of the ducks which die from it each year; in fact, so many ducks die each year in the U.S.A. that botulism is often called "western duck disease." Ferrets and mink may simply be found dead from an apparently inexplicable cause. Death can occur

171

in as short a time as half an hour, or it may take 24 hours. If an animal with this illness lasts longer than 36 hours after collapse, it stands a chance of recovery.

There are several types of *Clostridium botulinum* bacteria, the most usual being known as "type O." The bacterium is one of the most common known to science. Normally it is harmless, but if it comes into contact with decaying meat (all meat is in a state of decay from the moment of death) it produces as a by-product a toxin which is among the deadliest poisons known. The toxin affects the victim by attacking the joints in the nerve junctions and breaking them down, causing paralysis. This starts at the hind legs and creeps through the body until it affects either the diaphragm, causing death by suffocation, or the heart, causing death by heart failure. Once started there is no reliable cure. The affected animal starts looking fluffed up and dejected, soon losing the use of its hind legs, staggering and dragging its hind limbs as the paralysis takes hold. After a short time it is unable to move other than to lift the head. It becomes wasp-waisted and gasps for breath as the paralysis creeps up the body. It lies stretched out as if overheated, but if its temperature is taken it will be found to be several degrees below normal. All the while the animal will be dribbling from its mouth as it loses control of its ability to swallow; as it is unable to move, it will soil itself.

Ferrets are vulnerable to botulism because of their food and feeding habits. Raw meat is the trigger for the toxin. Even if it is not already affected when you give it to your stock, it may become so if there are already any bacteria in the cage—in the bedding, for example. If you have any suspicions about the meat you are about to feed, you must boil it thoroughly for ten minutes. When you are feeding meat that has been frozen, defrost it fast and feed it right away. If the meat has been infected beforehand, deep-freezing will kill many of the bacteria but not the spores,

As you can see, this ferret and its companion have great confidence in each other. You cannot expect to have a good rapport with your pet if you are afraid of it.

and if you leave it to defrost slowly you will give these spores a chance to produce fresh bacteria and, in turn, the toxin which will kill your stock. One self-appointed expert once told me that if you leave the meat to defrost for 12 hours the toxin will disperse. *This is not so.* Death can be caused by a very tiny amount, and because of this botulism will often pick off one animal in a group, which tends at first to cause some confusion. It is not an infectious disease—it cannot pass from one ferret to another, unless of course the dead animal is eaten by its companions, which is not likely.

When my own animals were dying of botulism I was desperately running around trying to find out what was killing them before I ran out of ferrets. After a lot of trouble and effort by all concerned, the cause was pinned down by the Ministry of Agriculture, Fisheries & Food vets at the Veterinary Investigation Department at Reading. They said right from the start just what the trouble was, but no one believed them; it took large blood samples from affected animals before proof was certain. I never discovered where the infection came from, but it seems most likely that the meat was infected at the source, in the slaughterhouse.

As I have already said, there is no reliable cure. There is a vaccine which offers protection against the bacteria, but unfortunately it does not appear to be readily available. In theory you can have your animals treated with an antiserum once the disease has been identified; the problem is that by the time you have identified the cause as botulism and made the antiserum, the animal is dead.

There are things which you can do in an attempt to keep the animal alive long enough for the body's natural repair processes to take over. Keep it warm and quiet, ideally placing it in a hay-filled box and laying it beside a hot-water bottle to keep its temperature up—a plastic screw-top bottle wrapped in a thick towel will suffice. Try to get the ferret to take food and water, especially water to combat dehydration. If the animal is unable to feed or drink you can feed it bread and milk slop or thin gruel by means of an endotracheal tube and syringe. Your vet will help with injections of antibiotics to keep pneumonia at bay.

VETERINARY NOTES

By now you will be well-aware that ferrets do not sicken and die of mystery diseases. Most of their troubles, if not all, are well-documented, and quite a few have been studied extensively. But the results of these studies rarely, if ever, filter down to the layman, and even veterinary surgeons do not always have ready access to all the basic information.

With this in mind, I include the following veterinary notes in the hope that they will be of interest and assistance to you in deciding what is normal and perhaps of some small assistance to your vet should he not often have to deal with ferrets.

The normal body temperature, taken at the rectum, is 38.8° C.

The heart rate, which is very high, is between 300 and 400 beats per minute.

The normal respiration rate is between 30 and 40 per minute.

The majority of antibiotics can be used quite safely on ferrets.

Administration of drugs can be carried out subcutaneously in the scuff of the neck, intramuscularly in the hind leg and intraperitoneally by injection into the cavity medial to the hind leg. There is no vein conveniently placed for intravenous injection. If you wish to give drugs by mouth, the animal should be held by the neck; the mouth will then open, allowing the use of a syringe or a dropper.

Should anesthesia be needed, the following agents can be used with relative safety:

Ketamine hydrochloride at 25 mg/kg intramuscularly produces deep stupor within ten minutes and can be supplemented by an inhalation agent in the form of 50/50 *nitrous oxide/oxygen* and 1-3% *halothane*. Recovery with the latter is very fast, and the animal can be on its feet in ten to fifteen minutes.

Alphaxalone-alphadolone at 12-15 mg/kg or *fentanyl citrate-fluanisone* at 0.5 mg/kg intramuscularly can be used to give light surgical anesthesia for 15 to 30 minutes. Muscular relaxation can be improved by the concurrent use of *xylazine hydrochloride* at 1.0 mg/kg.

If none of these agents is available, then *pentobarbitone sodium* can be given intraperitoneally at 36 mg/kg. Light anesthesia will develop in about ten minutes and last from 45 minutes to two hours. Recovery is slow, however—it may take several hours—and there is a danger of respiratory depression.

While placing some emphasis on the possible health problems of the ferret, if asked to sum up I would say: use common sense, good husbandry and reasonable care, and you will be rewarded with fit and healthy ferrets at home and reasonable bags of rabbits, commensurate with the numbers on the ground, when you take them to work.

Here are three bright-eyed pets. Ferrets are alert and curious animals. Should they become listless or refuse to eat, or should their fur "fluff up," they probably are sick, and a veterinarian should be consulted for advice.

The ferret's long, sinuous body, together with its agility, makes it a very adaptable animal for hunting—ferrets can easily slide down narrow rabbit holes. Above is a coffee-colored female.

The Canadian otter is a close relative of the ferret. Young otters,
like young ferrets, are very playful and entertaining.

Bibliography

Adams, R. *Watership Down*, Deutsch.

Bateman, J. A. *Animal Traps and Trapping*. David & Charles.

Bewick, Thomas. *A Natural History of British Quadrupeds*, W. Davidson.

Burton, Robert. *Carnivores of Europe*. B. T. Batsford.

Cooper, John. "Ferrets," from *A Manual of the Care and Treatment of Children's and Exotic Pets*. Edited by A. F. Cowie for the British Small Animals Veterinary Association.

Drabble, Phil. *Weasel in My Meatsafe*. Michael Joseph.

Everitt, N. *Ferrets: Their Management in Health and Disease*. Everitt.

Flowerdew, J. R. *Techniques in Mammalogy*. Mammal Review.

Hammond and Chesterman. *UFAW Handbook of the Care and Management of Laboratory Animals*. Churchill Livingstone.

Lever, Christopher. *Naturalised Animals of the British Isles*. Hutchinson.

Lockie, J. D. *Territory in Small Carnivores*. Symposia of the Zoological Society of London.

Lockley, R. M. *The Private Life of the Rabbit*. Deutsch.

Owen, Clifford. "The Domestication of the Ferret," from

The Domestication and Exploitation of Plants and Animals, by Ucko and Dimbleby. Duckworth.

Roser, R. J. and Laver, R. B. *Food Habits of the Ferret at Pukepuke Lagoon, New Zealand*. New Zealand Journal of Zoology.

Samuel, E. and Lloyd, J. Ivester. *Rabbiting and Ferreting*. British Field Sports Society.

Sheill, John. *Rabbits and Their History*. David & Charles.

Southern, H.N. *The Handbook of British Mammals*. Mammal Society.

Twigg, Graham. *The Brown Rat*. David & Charles.

The ferret shown above has sable coloring, one of the most common ferret colors. The body fur, tail and feet are dark brown, while the undercoat is beige. The mask across the face gives the ferret a raccoon-like appearance. Raccoons (opposite), however, are not in the same family as ferrets. They are in the family Procyonidae.

Index

Numbers in **bold** type denote photos.

A young jill nursing her kits.

Opposite: Taming your pet ferret requires time and patience, as with any animal. The ferret has very sharp teeth and may nip you if it is frightened or unsure of you. When handling your pet, be gentle yet firm so it becomes familiar with you and trusts you.

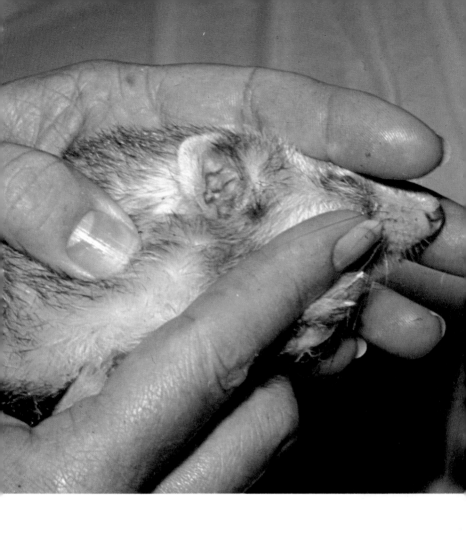

PS-792 FERRETS AND FER
RETING